Stock Trading + options trading

John Green

Contents

Introduction

Welcome to Stock Trading 101. In this book, we are going to discuss thirteen effective ways in which you can trade in the world of stocks with very little money. If you believe that such a thing is not possible, think again. The truth is that you don't need a great deal of money to make money in stocks. The adage, "it takes money to make money" is nothing more than a myth. The fact is that you can make money with little to no money. However, you need to know what you are doing.
That's what this book is all about.

This book is all about helping you find the best way to make money in stocks without having to break the bank. Moreover, you will find that it's quite simple and straightforward to get started. You don't need an advanced degree in finance. All you need to know are the secrets that insiders don't want you to know.
This is powerful stuff.

You see, insiders protect these secrets as much as possible because they want to sell you their most expensive products. This is why they tell you that you need to invest vast amounts of money. Additionally, they try to convince you that you can't make money as a small investor. They want you to think that you need to sink large amounts of money into their products. Why is this?

Simply put, they want you to keep sinking more and more money into their companies. But as you will see in this book, you don't even need to hire a stockbroker to manage your money. With the practical tips and strategies you'll learn in this book, you won't need to rely on a professional money manager. You'll get the knowledge you need to make money right away.

So, the time has come to get started. All you need is some time and effort put toward studying the information contained

herein. Ultimately, you will find that making money in this way provides you with the financial freedom you seek.
 Who knows, you may even find a way to rid yourself of debt and pesky debt collectors once and for all.

In the long run, the strategies contained in this book will enable you to create the type of life you have always dreamed of. The goal here isn't to have "X" amount of dollars in your bank account. The goal here is to create the type of life you have always want to live. This is about creating the lifestyle that you want for yourself and your loved ones. Perhaps that seems like a pipe dream at this point. But rest assured that it is entirely possible.

Others have done this, too. So now, it's time for you to make use of the knowledge that has enabled others to find financial freedom and build the life they have always wanted. So, let's get started on building the life you have always wanted. Stay tuned because things are going to get very interesting!

Chapter 1: Day Trading

If you are looking for a source of income that doesn't require you to work long hours or invest a great deal of money, then day trading could be a great choice. In day trading, you trade stocks employing a digital platform. The great thing about day trading is that you don't need to pay commissions to greedy brokers. This means that the money you make is yours. Your earnings and profits are yours. All you have to pay is a fee per trade and/or an annual subscription.

Unlike traditional investments in the stock market, you don't need a certain amount of capital to get started. With day trading, you can get started with as little as $500. You can get started by looking up discount brokers.

Getting a Brokerage Account

The first step to making money with trading is to set up a brokerage account. The best way is to ensure profit is through a discount broker. Regular brokers charge you an annual membership fee. Discount brokers don't normally charge fees. All they will ask you is to deposit your starting capital to begin. The way these companies make money is by charging you a fee per trade. The market rate is roughly $1.99 to $5.99. So, it pays to do some research before you sign up.

The next step is to look at the types of investment instruments that the platform offers. Ideally, you want to find a platform that offers you the widest range of stocks, ETFs, funds, and any other financial instrument. This is important as it will allow you to choose from various types of investments.

How to Make Trades

There are two ways of going about making trades. If you are keen on doing your research, you can check out companies to see which ones are coming up and which ones are going down.

Then, you can place your trades based on your perception of these stocks.

The other way you can make money is by following the pros. There are famous day traders who have made six-figures on day trading alone. These are the folks who have it down cold. So, you can learn from them. You can follow their lead and take the guesswork out of trading.

Renowned traders like Ross Cameron, Brett N. Steenbarger, Sasha Evdakov, and Rayner Teo have their sites, blogs, or YouTube channels in which they share their expertise. They can provide you with the guidance you need to make trades like the pros. Best of all, they offer free advice to their followers. Alternatively, you could pick up one of their books, or get a paid subscription, to their newsletters and bulletins.

About Trading Platforms

Choosing the right trading platform is the most important decision you can make when it comes to day trading. The right one will give you a good head start. Here are some things to consider as you choose the right one for you.
Additionally, always choose trading platforms that offer a free demo account. This type of account consists of free access to the trading platform for a limited time. Usually, you are granted access for 7 days, or as much as 30 days, to try out the platform. During this time, you are playing with monopoly money. This is the best opportunity you will ever have at learning the way day trading works without losing any of your own money. It is a simply fantastic way of learning the system before you go live for the real thing. That way, when you go live for real, you will hit the ground running.

Please keep in mind the golden rule of money management when day trading: never trade more than 2% of your investment in a single trade. For instance, you have $1,000 of investment capital, the most you should sink into a single trade should be

$20. The reason for this lies in the possibility of a deal going south unexpectedly. So, if you invest a large sum, then you'll be hit pretty hard. On the contrary, if you invest only 2%, you can afford to lose all of your investment. After all, it won't cripple your finances. Plus, you can offset these losses with the gains your make from other deals. In the end, you are covering your tracks.

High-Frequency Trading

For investors that are just starting, high-frequency trading, or HFT, is the best way they can build their way up. HFT consists of making small trades, with little profit, over and over again. The way you profit here is by the volume of transactions that you make. Consider this example:

You invest $100. You average a $5-profit on your trades. If you make 10 trades, you profit $50. If you make 20 trades, you profit $100. In short, the more trades you make, the more money you make. This is why HFT is the most effective strategy that day traders use when they start with little money.

Moreover, this is the reason why a discount broker makes sense. If you choose a broker that charges high transaction fees, your profits could be zapped by transaction fees. Thus, it makes sense to find a broker that allows you to make multiple trades.

Additionally, you can use analysts' picks to automate your trades. Therefore, you won't have to spend time looking for stocks to trade. You can use the recommended picks and go from there. By using this strategy, you can quickly make $50 or more per day.

If you are looking to make as much money as you can in the short term using the HFT strategy in day trading can provide you with the alternative you seek. Please bear in mind that it's best to close up your position before the end of the trading day. This will reduce your exposure to risk. Leaving positions open for longer than a trading day makes you vulnerable to market swings. As a result, it's a good idea to close up shop at the end of the trading day.

Chapter 2: Trading Options

One of the alternatives to trading regular stocks, such as in day trading, is options. Options are investment instruments that allow you to trade stocks but through minimizing risk. On the whole, options can provide you with the opportunity to make greater returns as compared to trading stocks only. Additionally, you can trade options as part of an ordinary day trading platform. You simply need to gain access to them.

Generally speaking, options are somewhat riskier than regular stocks as you need to anticipate the movements in the market. Therefore, they have earned a reputation for being dangerous. However, this reputation is due to improper use. Mainly, traders and investors who simply purchase options without doing their homework are vulnerable to risk.

Getting Started With Options

Most day trading platforms don't offer options trading right away. You sort of need to work your way up to it. It is possible to unlock them right away if you put up enough investment capital. However, this is not a good idea, at least not right away.

In general, there are two types of options: put and call options. First, a call option is an instrument that gives you the right to buy a stock but not the obligation to do so. With this type of option, you make a deal with sellers in which you agree to buy a stock if it meets certain criteria. If these criteria are met, you buy. However, some conditions allow you to back away from the deal should you choose to do so.

Next, a put option is essentially the opposite of a call option. This means that you have the right to sell the stock but not the obligation to do so. Generally speaking, you can sell once the deal reaches certain parameters. However, you can call off the deal should you choose to do so.

Now, let's consider how you can make money by using options. You are tracking a stock. It is currently trading at $12 a share. According to the experts, you follow, they feel the stock can reach $14 a share. But you are not comfortable with buying at $12. So, you set up your trade so that you buy at $11 and sell at $14. Should the stock's price fall to $11, the deal goes through. Then, you wait until the stock reaches $14 and automatically sell.

Advantages of Trading Options

There are clear advantages when it comes to trading options. Mainly, you get a leg up on trading stocks as compared to regular day trading. So, let's take a look at the biggest advantages that come from trading options:

- Options are more cost-effective
- Reduced risk
- Higher returns
- More alternatives

As you can see, options can provide you with a great way of trading stocks while minimizing risk. Furthermore, options can provide you with several advantages as compared to stocks alone. So, options are certainly an alternative to consider.

Setting Up a Successful Options Trade

Here is a great strategy that you can use to make money using options.
You are looking to purchase stock in DFT company. The current share price sits at $16 a share. Analysts believe that the stock will take off at any given point in time. So, you are eager to get in on the action. However, you feel that $16 is a bit high at the moment. As a result, you are not willing to buy at this price point.
On the flip side, it is extremely difficult to predict a possible pullback in the stock's price. Moreover, it is virtually impossible

to determine when the pullback may occur. This is where you decide to take out a call option on DFT.

To do this, you set up your trade so that you are prepared to purchase 100 shares at $14 a share. When the price dips and hits this target, the option is executed. You then purchase the stock. The transaction is closed, and you now own the stock.

The next part of this trade is to set up a put option. Since you anticipate that the DFT may go past $20 a share, you take out your call option at $21. Then, you sit and wait. Eventually, the stock hits your price point, the put option is executed, and you receive the proceeds.

The spread between the call and put options is your profit. The only cost associated with these transactions is the cost of the option itself. Depending on the issuing institution that you work with, this cost can be pennies on the dollar.

The best part of trading options is that they are fully automated. This means that all you need to do is set up your trade on your platform and sit back. Investors that don't have time to sit at their computer choose options. These provide them with the flexibility they need to go about their usual business. Therefore, options trading can become a great additional source of revenue.

Buy and Selling Options Contracts

The contracts themselves can be bought and sold. This deal consists of selling a standing contract to purchase or sell stocks. These transactions are coming when investors short a stock. A short sale consists of selling a stock you do not own. So, some investors are willing to buy options contracts when the stock itself is in short supply. As a result, you can make money simply by selling the contract itself.

The way to make money in this deal is to attach a premium to the contract. For instance, if the contract is valued at $100, you can add a $10 premium on the contract. This is a price that you set based on the conditions of the deal. If the buyer is desperate, they will pay. Generally speaking, investors are willing to pay these premiums, particularly when they are faced with a margin call. So, buying and selling the contracts themselves could prove profitable if you hold them in companies whose stock is in short supply.

Chapter 3: Investing in ETFs

Exchange-traded funds, or ETFs, allow investors to get a piece of the action without having a substantial investment capital. Often, these instruments allow small investors to gain exposure to a given market without the need to invest directly in it.

ETFs are instruments in which investors pool their money together. Then, a fund manager allocates that money in specific industries, assets, or markets. Then, the proceeds are distributed among the investors. Naturally, those who invest more get a larger share of the action.

The returns on ETFs are generally higher than your average high-yield savings account or mutual fund. They are designed to cover a myriad of markets. Thus, you can pick the one that's best for you given your objectives and interests.

Getting a Piece of the Action

Depending on the type of ETF you choose, you can get a share of the action without having to go all-in. For example, if you choose to invest in an oil ETF, you can gain exposure to the oil market without having to purchase oil contracts. This means you will make money on trading oil without having to purchase oil itself. Unless you are keen on having barrels of oil delivered to your door, an oil ETF is your best choice.

Other types of ETFs can be purchased for stocks, bonds, commodities, and currency. When you buy into an ETF, all you need to do is sit back and keep track of the fund's performance. To get into the action, you would need to do this through a broker. Since brokerage firms and financial institutions (such as banks) offer ETFs to their customers, you would need to visit them.

In many cases, there are funds that you can buy into with as little as $100. These funds also allow you to increase your stake by making monthly contributions. As your contributions grow, so do your profits. That's why they make a great choice when starting.

Great for Passive Investing

Passive investing means that you put your money to work without you actively managing it. As such, passive investing is great for folks, who are already working full-time or are unwilling to spend more time on other tasks. Thus, ETFs provide the opportunity to make money without having to invest more time and effort.

The neat thing about passive investing is that your money works for you while you spend your time elsewhere. This implies that you can continue to live your regular life while your account grows. And while you are exposed to the fluctuations of the market, the general trend is usually positive. So, if you stay in the fund long enough, you'll see positive results.

The "Buy and Hold" Strategy

ETFs won't make you rich overnight. But they will provide you with a solid source of income over time. If you are not keen on having an ETF produce income for you, rather you're keen on using it as a savings account, then you can be sure that you'll see your money grow.

For instance, some folks like to contribute money to an ETF when looking to save up for a down payment on a home. Once they have hit the target they seek, investors pull their money to purchase their home. In a way, you're trading one type of investment for another.

To do this, you need to be patient. Since time is a luxury, it's best to get started today. The longer you wait, the less time you'll have to reach your desired goals. Moreover, with the fluctuations in the market, you may see the value of your investment dip from time to time. This is why having time on your side makes all the difference.

Do Your Research

Not all ETFs are created equal. Some offer better returns than others. Also, some require larger investment capital. Most funds require you to keep your money invested for a certain period. This means that you cannot pull it unless you pay certain penalties. Naturally, that wouldn't make sense unless you needed the money.

Also, please make sure to check if the fund charges any maintenance fees. These might be part of the hidden costs that come with the fund. Most discount brokers don't charge any of these fees though they may hit you with an annual membership fee. Nevertheless, the majority of funds won't charge you any fees as long as you keep a certain balance.

Another important consideration is the type of fund you choose. It's always best to choose a fund that trades an asset you understand. In this case, you can choose an "index fund." This type of fund tracks the major stock indices such as the S&P 500, the NASDAQ, or the Dow Jones. Other index funds track overseas markets such as those in Asia and Europe. These funds are rather straightforward. You make money if the market is up, and you lose money if the market is down.

Index funds are a great way for you to make higher profits as compared to mutual funds. Mutual funds pay a lower interest rate as they usually invested in a diversified basket of stocks. This means that you are dependent on the individual performance of the companies that make up the fund. And while mutual funds are better than nothing, index funds offer a greater opportunity for profit.

Taking the Plunge

If you're ready to take the plunge into an ETF, you can check out online alternatives. In these alternatives, you don't need to take a trip down to your local broker. You can set up an online account, fund it, and then choose the type of ETF you wish to buy into. Then, you can sit back and watch your money grow over time. Of course, it's always good to make sure you are dealing with reputable institutions. However, most major financial corporations offer some kind of online ETF plan. Hence, you have plenty of options at your disposal.

Chapter 4: All About Penny Stocks

You may have heard of the term "penny stocks" thrown around in financial literature. These types of stocks are the subject of much speculation. However, most investors don't understand penny stocks. Moreover, you'll hear some folks dismiss penny stocks calling them a "waste of time."

If you play your cards right, you can make money on penny stocks without needing to invest a great deal of money. In essence, penny stocks consist of companies whose shares trade for under $5 a piece. The term "penny" was coined from the days in which some stocks traded for less than a dollar apiece. Since then, the term has been expanded to cover any stocks that trade below the $5 threshold.

It's also important to note that most penny stocks are companies that have been de-listed from major stock exchanges. Consequently, you will find these stocks in the "Over the Counter" (OTC) market. This type of market means that you don't necessarily need to go through a major stock exchange to purchase these types of stocks. Therefore, you can purchase them directly from other traders. Still, most trading platforms contain capabilities designed to handle OTC transactions.

The Tiers of Penny Stocks

There are four tiers for penny stocks. These tiers correspond to the stock's share price and its overall outlook. Let's take a look at each one.

- **Tier 1**. These are stocks that are traded on major stock exchanges such as the NASDAQ. Shares are valued at, or below, $5 a share. These stocks are considered to a higher value as they are held to the same standards as all other publicly-traded stocks. This means these companies must submit their financials in addition to any other regulatory requirements.

- **Tier 2**. These stocks are very much like tier 1 stocks except that they trade at or below $1.
- **Tier 3**. These shares trade for less than a cent. These stocks are not traded on any major stock exchanges as they have most likely been de-listed.
- **Tier 4**. These are known as "triple zero" stocks. As such, they are the subject of "hot penny" stock alerts. Since their valuation is so low, any slight movement in their valuation may lead to a potentially significant gain.

At first glance, penny stocks seem like a great way to make money. In this regard, penny stocks should be seen as a low cost, low reward proposition. This means that they won't cost you much, but you won't make a boatload of profits unless you invest a sizable amount. Herein lies the dilemma.

If you mainly deal with tier 1 and tier 2 stocks, then you have a good chance to make considerable profits. However, dealing with tier 3 and tier 4 penny stocks may produce underwhelming results. Still, you can make money especially if you aren't keen on buying shares of blue-chip companies.

How to Pick the Best Penny Stocks

By nature, penny stocks are volatile. This means that their valuation can climb just as quickly as it can fall. Therefore, you need to keep an eye out for companies that have the potential to generate a profit over time.
Here are some helpful tips:

- First, check out the company's financials. If they are making money, then you can assume the stock will be profitable. If the company is losing money, then you have a bad investment on your hands.
- Next, look at the company's debt. Most publicly-traded companies get de-listed because they run into trouble with their debt. They rack up too much debt and then cannot get out from under it. If you spot that the

company is under too much debt, then it's best to move on.

- Last, check out the company's strategy. It could be that the company fell on hard times and is working its way back into the good graces of stock exchanges. So, if you can see a good strategy in place, then there is a pretty good chance the stock will rebound.

In general, making use of a stock screener can help you narrow the playing field. Since there is a considerable amount of penny stocks out there, it can be pretty tedious to go through them one by one. So, using a stock screener with the characteristics you are looking for will help you save time. Then, you can go through each one to determine which ones are the best kind.

How to Make Money With Penny Stocks

Generally speaking, you can make money by either flipping these stocks in a short time for a smaller profit or hold on to them for a while longer in the hope of maximizing your return. Both of these strategies can work well, but there are a couple of things to keep in mind.

First, if you are not keen on holding on to penny stocks for an extended time frame (more than a day or two), then you can make good returns by engaging in high-frequency trading. This means that you make multiple trades over and over, in a short time window, thereby multiplying small gains.

Also, you can hold on to these stocks as long as you need to until they reach your expectations. This strategy is a bit more dangerous as it exposes you to potential crashes in share prices, particularly if the stock still has room to fall.

That being said, please keep in mind that the cheapest of the penny stocks are not always the most attractive options. Sure, they may be dirt-cheap, but they may not have any kind of upside whatsoever. So, you may find yourself possibly losing money as opposed to making it.

Lastly, here are three quick tips to help you pick the right penny stocks:

- Check out the news. If you find good news surrounding the company, such as a new product launch, then the stock could rise.
- Look at the number of outstanding shares. In general, the lower the number of outstanding shares the more potential for an increase in price.
- Keep an eye on trading volume. If you see that traders are buying and selling a particular stock, it might be a sign that it's poised to shoot up in value.

Chapter 5: Rolling Over Investments

It is said that you need money to make money. This belief stems from the idea that you invest a sum of money, and the proceeds then become a source of income. On the whole, this is a perfectly fine strategy. Of course, you need a sizable chunk of investment capital to make it work. Needless to say, this doesn't work well for those who don't have said investment capital.

Also, you need to ask yourself why you are investing in the first place. You see, most folks begin investing because they have a goal in mind. For instance, they are looking to save up for a down payment on a property, fund their retirement, or build the wealth they can pass on. All of these objectives, among others, are what motivate people to invest.

But one strategy that's commonly overlooked is known as "rolling over investments." This strategy is perfect for those who are starting small. Although, it should be noted that it's not the type of strategy that will build immediate wealth. But it does is create a snowball effect that will eventually pay off in the long run. All you need is a little patience.

Rolling over investments consists of investing a certain amount and then reinvesting the entire amount over and over again without withdrawing the proceeds from the original investment. In other words, you reinvest your principal plus interest. This is what creates the snowball effect.

The Snowball Effect in Action

Let's assume you start by opening a high-yield savings account and fund it with $100. Let's also assume that the bank pays you 1% monthly. This means that after the first month, you would have $101 (principal plus interest). Now, instead of withdrawing the $1 as income (on which you would have to pay taxes), you choose to roll it over for the next month. Now, the bank calculates your interest payout over $101 as opposed to $101. At the end of the following month, you have $102.01. The next month, you would roll over $102.01 and make $103.03. Do you see how the snowball effect takes place?

Sure, these numbers are underwhelming. However, they serve to illustrate how the snowball effect occurs when you choose to roll over your investments. This is a great strategy, particularly when you are not looking to make immediate use of the money.

How Much Should Be Invested

That depends on two factors.
First, it depends on how much money you can set aside. For most folks, money is tight. So, they may not be able to part with $1,000 to put away in a high-yield savings account, mutual fund, or ETF. Often, most folks start with less than $100. Ultimately, it doesn't matter how much money you start with. What matters is that you get started in the first place. Over time, you can add more funds to your investment and keep rolling it over. This makes the snowball effect grow even further.

Second, it depends on your aims. For most folks, investing is a means to an end. This means that they are not investing in the joy of investing. Rather, they invest because they are looking to get something out of it. As such, they may not have an immediate need for this money. If that's the case, then rolling over your investments can be a great strategy for you.

Additionally, rolling over investment works well for those who are looking to build an additional fund. This fund isn't destined to cover expenses or finance the acquisition of other goods. Rather, it serves as a savings fund, part of a retirement strategy, or simply as a means of protecting wealth. Thus, rolling over your investments makes perfect sense.

Investment Instruments to Consider

This boils down to your choice of an active or passive investment approach. A very common approach is to set up a passive investment scheme in which you open up any type of investment accounts such as a certificate of deposit, high-yield investment account, mutual fund, ETF, index fund, or money market account. Then, you put up your initial investment capital and simply let it roll over month after month. Depending on the type of account, you can add more funds to it whenever you can.

This last point is important as some accounts don't require much to open, sometimes as little as $25, but they do ask for monthly deposits. This is important to note as you may get penalized if you don't make the contributions. If you do choose this type of account, make sure that the monthly contribution is something you can comfortably. Also, automate your contribution, so you don't even have to think about it.

Rolling Over Investments as a Tax Strategy

An overlooked aspect of investing is that you are on the hook for taxes on your profits. Any time you collect interest, you are liable for capital gains tax. Depending on the type of approach you are investing in, you may also be liable for income tax.
So, one of the best ways to bypass the entire tax song and dance is to roll over your investments. It's also worth looking into the specifics of the investment account you open. Some accounts require you to stay invested for at least three years. After the mandatory period, you can withdraw your money tax-free. Depending on the nature of the account (and the balance), you can pull out sooner or must stay in longer.
In the case of 401(k)s or IRAs, you can't withdraw them until you are officially eligible to retire. So, if you have one of these plans, particularly through your employer, then just let that money roll over and over. In the end, you'll stand to benefit a great deal once you are eligible to withdraw it tax-free.

It is certainly worth using rollovers as a means of minimizing your tax burden. After all, you work hard for your money. So, you should be able to keep as much of it as you can.

Chapter 6: Investing in Precious Metals

Every time there's talk of a recession or economic downturn, you hear about gold. This discussion centers on gold (along with other precious metals such as silver), being a hedge against downturns in stocks and other financial assets.

Indeed, gold is a hedge against downturns. This is mainly due to the inverse correlation between stocks and precious metals. The rationale is that when investors are uncertain about stocks, they pull their money from the stock market and sink into gold.

Aside from gold, silver, palladium, and platinum are all considered investment-grade precious metals. These have a wide range in prices making them somewhat unaffordable for investors that are just starting. This is why many folks look to silver as it is the cheapest of these metals. Additionally, silver tends to outperform gold. This means that when silver spikes, it short through the roof.

How to Make Money With Precious Metals

Firstly, you can buy physical and then sell for a profit. This is like buying and selling any other commodity. However, you need to be careful as buying and selling precious metals in pawnshops is not the best idea. So, this means dealing with a reputable precious metals dealer. These companies will happily buy-back your metals at a higher price. It all depends on the "spot" price, which is the metal's current market valuation.

However, you may find buyers that are desperate for physical metals. At this point, you can charge whatever you want for your position. This is why establishing a good relationship with a reputable dealer can turn into a profitable proposition when you are looking to sell your physical metal.

Secondly, ETFs provide you with exposure to the action, with much less risk, and none of the stress. You make money if the price of gold goes up. You lose money if the price goes down.

Depending on the nature of the fund, you'll get a check for your proceeds every quarter. Alternatively, you can ask your broker to rollover your proceeds. This makes your stake in the fund grow while avoiding any taxes on your earnings.

Making Money by Selling Your ETFs

In some instances, investors may be actively seeking to get into precious metals. However, sellers of physical metals may be in short order. So, investors would then flock to ETFs. This commonly occurs during economic downturns.

To make money in this situation, you can simply sell your stake in the ETF, not for the money you have invested, but rather for the amount of money you stand to make.
Consider this situation:

You have invested $100 in a gold ETF. Investors are looking to buy into the fund you are invested in. So, you can sell your position for $200. The reason for this additional premium is that other investors are buying what your stake will be worth eventually, not what it is worth today. Investors are willing to pay this additional premium in desperate times when stocks are falling. Please bear in mind that precious metals generally go in the opposite direction of stocks. So, when the stock market is tanking, your precious metals position should increase in value.

Physical or Paper?

There are two ways of owning precious metals.
The first is physical. This means that you purchase your metals and have them delivered to your home or office. This is called "allocated" ownership. The advantage is that you have complete ownership of your metals. Thus, you are the sole proprietor. The downside is storing them in your home. This can get pricey. Besides, homeowner's insurance doesn't usually cover gold unless you add it to the policy.

The second is "paper." Paper gold means that you don't take physical ownership of the metal. All you are doing is gaining exposure to the market without ever getting ownership of the coins or bars. So, you pool your money, along with other investors, while a fund manager invests it in the metal. You then get a check every quarter for your earnings. This can be done through ETFs or gold investment accounts. The same can be done for the other precious metals. Alternatively, you can invest in a precious metals fund. This fund is diversified in all metals, thereby giving you access to all metals at once.

Beware of Premiums

When you buy physical metal, you must pay a premium. The premium is the amount of money paid on top of the spot price. This charge is issued to cover the dealer's expenses, overhead, and so on. Depending on current market conditions, premiums can range from a couple of dollars over the spot price to several hundred. It all depends on the price per ounce and the demand for it. Do your homework and shop around to get the best price.

It should be noted that when you buy into an ETF, there are no premiums to be paid as you are not purchasing the physical metal. Therefore, these premiums are not part of the contract. This makes your investment capital go further.

Precious Metals as Part of Wealth Preservation

There is a lot of discussions surrounding precious metals as a means of preserving wealth. If you are looking for a long-term investment, then this is the one for you. To preserve wealth, it makes sense to own physical bars and coins. The rationale behind this is that money loses purchasing power over time due to inflation. In the case of precious metals, their valuation keeps up with inflation as they are repriced over time. This means that the valuation of your metals goes up over time due to inflation. Thus, you get more money for the same amount of metals.

Precious metals can also be passed from generation to generation. So, it makes sense to keep them for a long time as coins and bars will not deteriorate with time. This is why they make great gifts. Plus, they are highly liquid. This means that they can be easily sold.

Chapter 7: FOREX and Currency Markets

FOREX is one of the hottest markets at the moment; it is a dynamic, fast-paced environment. It is also the world's only 24-hour market. This means that you can trade on the FOREX market at any time you want. So, it's perfect for those individuals who are looking to make money in addition to their regular jobs. Moreover, those who make a living from trading FOREX have the opportunity to build a flexible schedule.

In essence, the FOREX market boils down to buying and selling currency. It's very similar to day trading, but instead of trading stocks, you're trading currency. Beyond that, the fundamentals are essentially the same. In general, the "buy low/sell high" logic applies here, as well. So, it's a question of playing the markets based on your expectations.

How Does FOREX Work?

Here is a sample FOREX deal you can make right away.
Let's take a look at a winning trade. In this trade, we're going to trade the currency pair USD/GBP. So, you are holding GBP and buy USD.

Here is the cross rate: USD stands at 0.84950 while the GBP sits at 0.84960.
Now, you decide to buy $10,000 as a part of the trade. Additionally, the USD/GBP pairing holds a margin rate of 3.34%. This is important as you are not required to come up with the $10,000 upfront. Rather, you only need 3.34%, in other words, you need to deposit $340 to finalize the deal.

Next, you need to sell your position before you get a margin call. This is why FOREX moves very fast. The longer you hold on to a trade, the greater your exposure to risk. Thus, you need to be keen at which point you stand to make a profit. When you hit this point, you can sell for a profit.

In our example, the price shifts to 0.85540 for the GBP. So, when you sell, you stand to make about $15 on the trade. The result is profitable as you invested $340 and made $15 on the trade. This is a 4.4% return.

HFT in FOREX

Based on the previous example, you can make good money on FOREX by engaging in HFT. To make this work, you need to make multiple trades throughout a trading session. In short, the more profitable trades you make, the more money you earn.

Since FOREX is a 24-hour market, you don't need to trade at a specific time of day. You can trade at any time you free. There is no cap to the number of trades you can make in a session. So, if you make 10 successful trades at $15 a piece, you can make $150 in a session. If you amplify that by 100 trades, you can make $1,500.

This is why HFT is the preferred approach to FOREX. Moreover, the name of the game is automation. By automating your trades, you can make multiple trades in short order. The only time you need to invest in setting up your trades. Once you have them all in line, then you are ready to hit the ground running. As a result, FOREX is a great way in which you can make profits with very little money upfront.

How to Get Started in FOREX

Like day trading, you need to find a brokerage institution to grant you access to their trading platform. Some institutions specialize exclusively in FOREX, while others may offer you access to FOREX through a regular day trading platform. Ultimately, it's a good idea to find a day trading platform that allows you to trade FOREX. That way, you won't have to deal with multiple platforms. You'll be able to trade in a single platform across various markets. Additionally, this type of approach will allow you to learn on the system and perfect your strategy.

As for strategy, you can follow the top moneymakers in the FOREX world. These individuals post their picks on their sites. So, you can get free picks. Dailyfx.com is a great place to start. Their daily picks provide valuable insight. As a result, you don't need to put in hours and hours of research. You can follow their analysts' recommendations and place your trades accordingly.

Also, it pays to look into the amount of capital you need to fund your account. Most FOREX accounts can be opened with as little as $500. It's not a prohibitive amount though it may be a bit much for some at first. This is why tying your day trading account with a FOREX one can help you avoid this requirement. You might not be able to trade FOREX right away, but you are generally granted access to it after a trial period.

FOREX ETFs

For those who favor a more passive approach, there are FOREX ETFs you can look into. They usually pay a higher yield as compared to other types of ETFs. However, these ETFs don't offer too many options. Therefore, you essentially invest your money and go along for the ride. Depending on the nature of the fund, you may be asked to keep your money in for several months before even seeing your first check. Unfortunately, FOREX traders take a lot of risks. Thus, they don't generally commit to making periodic payments or assign a fixed rate of return.

Nevertheless, FOREX ETFs can make sense for you if you are looking for a way to diversify your investment portfolio while trying to get away from stocks, bonds, or even precious metals. The great thing about FOREX ETFs is that they don't require a lot of money upfront and allow you to contribute to the fund in a pay-as-go scheme. In the end, you get a great deal of flexibility.

On the whole, FOREX offers investors a great opportunity to make money in a very short time frame. So, if you are looking to make immediate returns, check out FOREX. While it won't make you rich overnight, it will provide you with the income you may need to cover your expenses in the short term.

Chapter 8: Cryptocurrency Trading

Cryptocurrencies (or cryptos) are the latest investment that you can take advantage of. On the surface, the concept of crypto is rather straightforward. You can make money from trading crypto just like you would FOREX.

It should be noted that Bitcoin is not the only game in town. So, if you are keen on getting in on the action, there are thousands of other coins to choose from. Some cost pennies on the dollar. Hence, you can find some good value options.
So, let's take a look at how you can make money through investing in crypto with little upfront money.

Buy and Hold

The "buy and hold" strategy is one of the most common ways in which you can invest your dollars. This strategy consists of buying up crypto and holding on to it for an extended time frame. It should be pointed out that the crypto is not nearly as dynamic as the FOREX one. So, this means that you can't expect to day trade crypto and have the same results. Often, investors in crypto find themselves holding their positions open for several days, if not weeks before they see movements in price action. When this occurs, they can sell.

So, the buy and hold strategy makes sense especially if you are looking to park some money that you don't need right away. However, there is one thing to look out for: the crypto market is highly volatile. This means that price changes can happen very rapidly. As a result, you could find your holding shoot up in value at a moment's notice. This is true of cryptos like Litecoin and Ethereum.
It is not recommended that trade in Bitcoin as its valuation is prohibitive for most investors.

Investing in Crypto ETFs

Crypto ETFs are a great way to get in on the action especially when you don't have much money to start with. For some investors, purchasing a single Bitcoin can be prohibitive. Considering that Bitcoin's price ranges from $10,000 to $12,000 per coin, purchasing individual coins can cost a pretty penny. So, crypto ETFs provide investors with exposure to Bitcoin without shelling out the big bucks.

Making money with ETFs is pretty straightforward. You buy into the fund and see returns based on the amount you invest. The great way about making from crypto ETFs is that price can shoot through the roof at a moment's notice. As such, you can reap the rewards.

While ETFs are a passive approach, you can certainly make money over time by rolling over your earnings. Please make sure you are aware of the fund's rules as you may not be able to withdraw your money for some time. So do keep this in mind.

Trading Cryptos for Profit

This is the most straightforward way that you can make money with cryptos. In this strategy, you buy low and sell high. That's pretty much all there is to it. This is a more active approach and certainly favored by investors looking to maximize their earnings.

To make money from this strategy, you can start with cheaper coins. For instance, Litecoin trades about $50 to $60 a coin. This might seem appealing to you if you have about $1,000 that you can invest in. In that case, even a $1 increase in price would easily land you $100 profit straight up.

However, for some investors, $1,000 isn't realistic. So, there are even cheaper coins, like Tether. This coin trades at about $1 a piece. It's a great coin to get started. If you are looking for something even more affordable, XRP trades at about 30 cents per coin. With $100, you can buy a good chunk of this coin.

Realistically, you can make small profits in the early going. As the price increases, you can then turn around and make a decent profit. With a coin such as XRP, a gain of about 10 cents would make you a healthy return.

Consider this situation:

You have $100 to spend on cryptos. So, you buy roughly 330 XRP coins at 30 cents apiece. Now, let's assume the price goes up to 35 cents per coin. When you sell your entire lot, you receive $116. That's $16 profit on a single trade. Percentage-wise, that's a 16% return.

That's not a bad place to start.

High-Frequency Trading

From the previous example, you can engage in high-frequency trading. To make money in high-frequency trading, you essentially make smaller trades many times over. So, if you make $16 in a single trade, and multiply that by 5, you could easily make $80 in a single trading session. Of course, this is assuming that you can pull this off five times a day.

In this example, we mention five times a day though it could be more. The great thing about cryptos is that there is a vast number of cryptos out there. So, you wouldn't necessarily make money from the same crypto over and over. Rather, you could make five separate trades in different coins. This would allow you to cash in several times a day.

Over time, you will learn the market so well that you'll know which coins to trade and when to trade them. In the end, you'll be able to build a steady stream of income.

Rolling Over Your Earnings

Just like with other types of investments, you can simply roll over your earnings. This will allow you to build up a greater amount of investment capital. As such, you'll be able to place bigger and bigger trades. This, in turn, would help you generate greater profits in every trade. Ultimately, you will have the chance to generate enough income on a daily, weekly, or monthly basis to where you can rely on it. This stream of income is potentially unlimited. So, you can't put a cap on how much you can earn.

Please bear in mind that lots of crypto investors like to combine high-frequency trading with the buy and hold strategy. In doing so, you'll be maximizing your earning potential.

Chapter 9: Shorting Stocks

Investors say a lot about shorting stocks. Many investors claim that it's too hard or too dangerous to pull off a successful short. This is true if you don't know what you are doing. However, if you have done your homework, you can make it work.
So, let's take a look at how you can pull off a successful short sale.

The Setup

Trade setup for a successful short depends on the direction a stock is trending. So, it's a matter of timing rise and the fall in price. It's not quite as hard as it sounds. But it does require you to be familiar with the stock's overall behavior.
To line up a good setup, you need to observe the price action of the stock in question. Ideally, it should be trading in a range. That way, you have a predictable range on which you can base your setup. Since shorting a stock consists of selling it before you own it, you need to be sure that the price will rise to a certain point and then fall back down.

When you are certain of these points, you can then move on to making the trade happen. The easiest way to determine if a stock is trading in a range is to observe its trendline. If you see the trendline moving sideways, then you know it's trading in a range. As such, all you need to figure out is where the resistance and support levels lie.

Making the Sale

Once you have identified the range in which the stock is trading, the next step is to set up the sale. To make the short happen, you need to set up the sale first. This can happen by either buy an option or responding to the request of another trader that is looking to purchase that particular stock.

Next, you execute the trade under the conditions of the buyer. It should be noted that you will have a specific timeframe to deliver ownership of the stock. During this window, you need to purchase the stock. That way, you will own the number of shares needed to fulfill your end of the deal.

At this point, the success of the trade hinges on the price falling within the time window you have to deliver the stock. If this happens, you'll be able to buy at a lower price, thereby generating you a profit. Should the price not fall, then you will still be on the hook for the stock. However, you'll have to buy it at whatever price it's available. Needless to say, you stand to lose money.

Making the Purchase

To make your purchase, you can set up an option based on the price you expect the stock to fall. If, and when, the stock falls to the level you expect, you'll be able to purchase it at a lower price than the agreed price. At this point, you can confidently buy the stock, deliver it to your buyer, and keep the difference.
If the price should not fall to a point where you can generate a profit, you can either cancel the sale (you can cancel the option) or go through with the trade and absorb the loss. Depending on the nature of the option, you may not be able to back out. So, you'll have no choice but to go through with the trade at a loss. It's also important to note that if you fail to deliver, you could have your account suspended for a given amount of time, or you might be kicked off the exchange altogether. So, it's best to play by the rules in this type of trade.

Making a Profit

As you can see, making a profit is all about selling when the stock's price is at its highest point and then purchasing the actual shares when the price falls back down. The difference between the purchase and the selling price is your profit.

It should be noted that you don't need to have any money when shorting stocks. This is why it's quite risky to engage in this strategy. If the price did not fall to where you expect it to, it would mean that you need to cover the difference from your funds. If you don't have enough funds, your account will be suspended.

If all goes well, you'll receive the proceed from the sale of the stock. Then, you can take these proceeds and purchase the stock at a lower price. Thus, you have enough funds to cover the spread. Many professional stock traders short stocks as this allow them to maximize the number of trades they make in a given period. Since they don't necessarily need to have the money to make trades happen, they can make multiple trades at once.

Sample Trade

Let's consider an example.
You are looking to short STX. This stock has been trading in a range between $10 and $15 a share. You find an investor has taken out an option to purchase 100 shares. So, you make a deal with the investor to deliver 100 shares. At the time of the trade, you agree to deliver the shares at $15 each. That's $1,500 that you receive from the sale.

The next step is to locate 100 shares of STX. So, you take out an option to purchase the 100 shares at $11 each. Another trader shows up and offers you the 100 shares at the price you requested. Thus, you make the deal, purchase the 100 shares for $1,100. Lastly, you deliver the shares to the first investor with whom you made the deal. You close the deal and keep $400 in profits.

In this example, it's evident that these types of deals can be made with no money. However, it's highly recommended that you do not short stocks you are not familiar with. Only short stocks you are very familiar with as you can ascertain where their price movements will go. This will save you a lot of headaches down the road.

Chapter 10: Using a Robo-Advisor

In the age of automation, leveraging technology to your benefit is a must. Most of the trading in the stock market is done through computer algorithms and artificial intelligence. As such, that technology has made its way into the mainstream. So, it's no longer available to just big-time traders. Now, regular investors can take advantage of these incredible tools.

In this chapter, we're going to be looking at Robo-advisors and how these can help you maximize your profits.

The Science of Robo-Advisors

In essence, a Robo-advisor is a piece of fancy computer code that makes trades for you. Since there is no human interaction involved, the Robo-advisor can work for you as much as you want it to. You don't have to worry about it burning out or coming down with stress. It'll get the job done whenever you need it to.
The biggest advantage of a Robo-advisor is that it requires very little maintenance once it's up and running. So, it doesn't cost much to make use of it; also, Robo-advisors have the luxury of processing vast amounts of information in a short time. Therefore, you can trust that it will make a smart decision based on available data. Of course, they're not perfect, but Robo-advisors do have a much better track record than human traders.

Also, Robo-advisors can help you hit the ground running. This means that you can set up your account and start trading in a matter of minutes. As a result, you'll start seeing profits immediately. This means that all you need is to have your investment capital ready to go.

Cost of a Robo-Advisor

Naturally, a Robo-advisor is not free. In some cases, a Robo-advisor may cost around $25 a year. That's an incredibly low fee, especially when compared to the fees that stockbrokers charge. In some cases, your Robo-advisor may charge you a fee of 0.25% to 0.50% on the total balance of your account. So, it pays to check out the terms of the account you are looking to open.

Additionally, trading with a Robo-advisor cost less than regular day trading. In day trading, you generally pay a fee per transaction. With Robo-advisors, brokerage institutions don't generally charge transaction fees. As a result, you make money on your deals without paying some of that back in transaction fees. That's why you either pay an annual fee or a fee on your account balance.

Getting Started With a Robo-Advisor

Mainly, Robo-advisors deal with regular investment accounts such as the kind you open for day trading. Other types of Robo-advisors manage index funds or individual retirement accounts. They may even help you with your 401(k) portfolio. However, the bulk of Robo-advisors deal with individual trading accounts.

Some Robo-advisor accounts have a minimum requirement upwards of $10,000. These types of accounts deal in specific markets and instruments. However, most Robo-advisors have very small account minimums. In some cases, you can open them for $500 or less. That's why it's important to check out various types of accounts.

Once you have selected your account provider, the Robo-advisor will assess your goals and risk tolerance. This is generally done by filling out a questionnaire. Depending on the nature of the Robo-advisor, it can be more or less thorough. Based on the information you provide it; its trading algorithm will adjust its performance to suit your specifications.

Once the algorithm has been set up, the Robo-advisor will begin by selecting instruments, stocks, and other assets to fund your portfolio. Generally speaking, the Robo-advisor's algorithm will seek out the best choices among low-cost ETFs, index funds, or specific stocks such as those traded in the S&P 500. In other cases, it may copycat other algorithms. This occurs when multiple algorithms are interacting with one another across various platforms.

What to Expect From a Robo-Advisor

If you already have a portfolio, you can enlist the services of a Robo-advisor to help you manage it. Often time, balancing your portfolio is about managing risk, or find a balance among the various types of asset allocations. Robo-advisors are good a diversifying your investments. As such, you can feel confident that your overall portfolio, regardless of your total amount invested, will respond to healthy parameters.

For instance, if your portfolio is invested fully in stocks, your Robo-advisor may whittle your stock allocation down to 25%. The remaining 75% may be spread out across other types of assets such as ETFs, index funds, commodities, or FOREX. Ultimately, you determine the parameters the trading algorithm will follow based on your expectations.

Additionally, Robo-advisors are good at maximizing your tax-strategy. If you are looking for ways to help you manage your tax bill, Robo-advisors can provide you with a customized approach. Again, this depends on your specific parameters. Ultimately, you can get the right allocation based on your preferences.

A Hybrid Approach

In some cases, a mix of a Robo and human advisor can provide you with a solid two-pronged attack. This strategy is useful, particularly when you are looking to be a passive investor. It should be noted that this approach is generally reserved for individuals with a larger portfolio.

Generally speaking, a hybrid approach is reserved for investors who have at least $25,000 worth of investable assets. Companies like Charles Schwab, Vanguard, and Facet Wealth all offer these services. Nevertheless, you can check out the strictly Robo-advisor services. They start with as little as $500 in investment capital. If you choose to roll over your earnings, you can build up your investment capital in short order. This is important to note as Robo-advisors tend to outperform the market. So, it's worth considering.

Lastly, the use of a Robo-advisor is a good strategy when you are looking to combine it with other investment approaches. For instance, you can combine your Robo-advisor along with day trading. Please bear in mind that the more income streams you can generate, the better your overall portfolio will be. So, Robo-advisors are a low-risk, high-reward proposition you should look into.

Chapter 11: Trading With Acorns

Acorns is an automated investment fund. This fund was developed by a group of investors, Ph.D. economists, and software engineers to provide investors with an easy way of saving money for retirement. Since its inception, Acorns has grown to a one-billion-dollar fund. Needless to say, it has been quite successful.

Getting Started With Acorns

Acorns used the concept of "micro-investing." This means that you do not need a large amount of investment capital to get started. You can get started investing with Acorns with as little as a dollar. You can then add money to your account as you go. There are no account minimums and no fees. This is why Acorns is such a great alternative for those investors that don't have much money to invest.

Since Acorns is a fully automated system, all you need to do is set up your account. It takes about 5 minutes, and you're all set to go. The system takes care of the rest. Acorns invest its funds in a myriad of diversified assets. So, it's about as safe as stock investing can get.

Your Acorns Portfolio

Your Acorns portfolio is one large, collective portfolio that's shared among all of the other investors who are part of the fund. As such, both the risk and wealth are spread out among all of the investors in the fund. When you set up your account, you'll be asked to fill out a questionnaire much the same way a Robo-advisor does. This helps the trading algorithm determine the best options to build your strategy. Therefore, your returns are based on the amount of money you have invested. So, if you invest a dollar, your returns will be calculated on that dollar. Additionally, your rate of return will be based on your expectations. This makes Acorns a practical way of making money generate more money.

Acorns is a great way for you to get started with saving and investing with practically no money. You can get started with a dollar. However, it would be best if you could set aside a larger amount, say, $20 or even $50. Since it is a passive form of investing, all you need to do is set up your account and watch your share of the portfolio grow.

That's all there is to it!

Building on Your Initial Investment

Once you have made your initial investment, even if it's just a dollar, you can then add to your account as you go. Since there are no account minimums, you can add as much money as you can to your account. Acorns is about investing your spare change. This means that you can put as much money as you can into the fund. Additionally, there are no penalties if you don't add any more funds.

To make your investment grow, consider adding a fixed amount every week, or month, to your account. This will help your investment gain momentum. Since you can add as much, or as little, as you wish, Acorns gives you the flexibility of converting it into your digital piggy bank.

Rolling Over Your Earnings

The next step is to take your earnings and roll them over. Since micro-investing starts quite small, it's best to roll over your earnings on top of what you add to your account. This enables you to create a snowball effect. As the snowball grows, you'll be able to watch your funds generate more and more returns. As a result, you'll soon see your money growing like magic.

Please beware of a common mistake most novice investors make by pulling out their investment too soon. Often, investors get anxious and pull their money way too soon. In this case, their investment doesn't have the chance to snowball into a significant sum. As a result, they feel the investment wasn't worth it.

So, investing with Acorns is about putting spare change into the digital piggybank and then forgetting about it. Furthermore, you can automate deductions from your bank account. Given that there are no limits, you can automate as much as you want. This makes investing in Acorns even easier.

The Purpose of Investing in Acorns

Investing in Acorns is a great way of building an emergency or rainy-day fund. Lots of folks find themselves without a fund they can draw on in case of emergency. Since saving money in a regular piggybank doesn't generate any returns, it's can be tough to build a fund the old-fashioned way.

With Acorns, you can build your emergency fund very quickly, easily, and without any of the hassle. Before long, you'll have enough money set aside should you ever need it.

Consider this example:

If you invest a dollar, at a 5% monthly return, you'll ear a nickel on that dollar every month. That's a nickel you have earned by simply opening an account and depositing that dollar. The next month, you'll earn 5.25 cents just by rolling that one dollar over.

If we expand this example to $100, you'd be making $5 a month. By rolling over your investment, you stand to make $5.25 the next month, and so on. This is why it's best to leave your money in the account so you can allow it to gain momentum. As such, investing in this type of account is about starting small and letting your seed grow consistently. Eventually, you'll hit your target.

Over time, an investment account in Acorns can provide you with a significant source of income. Ultimately, this depends on your lifestyle. If you live a relatively modest lifestyle, it shouldn't be too tough to build a solid stream of income. While it may not pay for everything, it will certainly help you to supplement your overall income. At the end of the day, it can provide you with the opportunity to generate passive income. So, it is certainly worth taking a chance on Acorns. You'll be glad you got started in micro-investing.

Chapter 12: Investing in Index Funds

Index funds are another great passive investment. They provide investors with the opportunity to gain exposure to the stock market without trading in individual stocks. This is an important feature as it helps diversify risk. On the whole, index funds give investors exposure to an entire stock index, that is, a whole array of stocks. As a result, this diversification mitigates risk. This is the ultimate way of putting your eggs in various baskets.

Getting Started With Index Funds

The first step is to select the right fund for you. There are several funds. So, it's important to review them all before setting your sights on one.
Here is a list of the major ones:

- The Wilshire 5000
- The Russell 2000
- The NASDAQ Composite
- MSCI EAFE (mostly European and Asian stocks)
- The Dow Jones

There are also other smaller stock indices. The smaller ones tend to be custom-made products set up by financial corporations or hedge funds. They are pitched to individual investors or may represent a specific niche. You can look into these if you are keen on investing in a smaller fund. However, these funds may require higher investment capital. So, it's important to keep that in mind.
Index funds are pegged to a specific stock index. For instance, the Dow Jones groups the 30 largest companies in the United States. In comparison, the Wilshire 5000 is based on the 5000 largest corporations. This implies that there is a much broader selection of companies.

Making Money With Index Funds

Buying into an index fund can be done in one of two ways. The first way is through an online platform, such as in the case of day trading. In this case, you select your fund and buy into it. Depending on the fund, the minimum amount of investment capital will vary. In some cases, you can buy into the fund with as little as $200 or $300. With these funds, you'll find that they offer moderate returns. Roughly speaking, index funds perform at the market average. On the whole, you can expect a run of the mill fund to perform at around 6% a year.

That's much better than the returns you'd get on a regular high-yield investment account.

Thus, you make money as long as the market is up. If the market experiences a downturn, as you would expect to from time to time, then you may end up losing money. This is why index funds offer good value as they are invested across a wide range of companies and industries. Unlike industry-specific ETFs, index funds look to spread out your asset allocation as much as possible. This is how you can achieve these returns.

All About Fees

It should be noted that index funds come with fees attached. These fees are generally charged for account maintenance. This is true of funds which are managed by human money managers. Naturally, the institution issuing the fund needs to cover overhead. If you are keen on having a human money manager handle the fund, then this would be the best option for you.

However, there are index funds that are managed by Robo-advisers or trading algorithms. As such, they don't require any human interaction. These funds offer a great deal of value as they charge minimal maintenance fees. In some cases, they don't charge any fees at all. So, it's worth looking into an index fund managed by a Robo-advisor. Often, automated fund managers beat average market returns. So, this bodes well for you.

Setting Up Your Strategy

When you go about setting up your strategy, there are two possibilities.

The first is the "buy and hold" strategy. This is a long-term strategy that you can use if you aren't in a rush to make significant returns. This approach is highly passive and capitalizes on the snowball effect. In short, the longer you leave your investment intact, the more money you make. Also, you can simply roll over your investment every time the interest payout comes around. If your fund offers monthly payouts, then simply roll them over. If interest payments are quarterly, you might consider pulling a portion of it and rolling over the rest.

The great thing about the buy and hold strategy is that it doesn't take a whole lot to get started. You can begin with whatever the account minimum happens to be. Then, you can add more funds to the account as you can. Over time, you'll see your investment begin to take off.

The second approach is a much more aggressive one. In this approach, you open up your account with the minimum required. Then, you commit to putting as much as you can into the fund. However, you are not looking to buy and hold for the long haul. When you choose to take a more aggressive approach, you need to be ready to pull your money when the market is heading toward a recession. As a yardstick, the stock market enters "correction" territory when it's down at least 20% from its previous high. Needless to say, taking a 20% is not a good investment. Consequently, you need to be ready to pull your investment as soon as you see trouble ahead.

To facilitate your chances of pulling out ahead of time, you need to make sure that there are no time restrictions. Some funds may ask you to keep your money invested for a certain time frame. If this is the case, then you might be on the hook for a few months or even a few years. If the markets take a downturn during that time, you have no choice but to go along for the ride. However, if you have the freedom to pull your money as soon as trouble looms, you can do so freely. Then, you can reinvest once the crisis is over.

As you can see, index funds are a great way to enter a passive investment without having to make a significant upfront investment.

Chapter 13: Investing in Private Equity

When we refer to private equity, we're talking about taking an ownership stake in a private company. This means that you are not buying stock from a company that's traded on the stock market. Rather, you are investing in individual companies such as startups.

Investing in private equity generally involves funding a new company or providing startup capital. In most cases, this requires a significant investment, often thousands of dollars. Now, it's important to note that private equity means that you receive shares, or a stake, in a company in exchange for your cash.
So, let's take a look at how you can make money by investing in private equity.

Taking Part in Crowdfunding

Entrepreneurs turn to crowdfunding when they need capital. This capital can be used for any number of aspects related to the business. Since finding individual investors that can provide them with capital is hard, some entrepreneurs turn to crowdfunding.

In these crowdfunding campaigns, entrepreneurs usually offer incentives to their investors. For instance, they'll over limited-edition products. In other cases, entrepreneurs may choose to issue stock in exchange for funds. These are the types of opportunities you can take advantage of.

During some crowdfunding campaigns, entrepreneurs may put up a few thousand shares at a specific share price. Depending on the price, you can buy up a bunch of them. In other cases, shares may be so cheap that you can buy up a decent lot for a couple of hundred dollars.

Making money in this type of approach is rather straightforward. You can hold on to the stock until the company begins to expand and take off. At that point, you might get a buy-back offer from the founders of the company. At that point, you can sell for a profit. Otherwise, you can sell to other investors later on.

Taking Dividends

If you choose to hold on to the stock, you should be eligible to take dividends. Dividends are the portion of the profits that shareholders are entitled to. Since you were generous enough to invest your money in a given company, you should get a cut of the proceeds.

However, you need to be careful. Please ensure that the terms and conditions of the stock issue state that you are eligible for dividends. This is important to note as the terms may state that you would be eligible for dividends after a specific time frame. Therefore, you need to be aware of this before pledging your money.

Still, taking dividends can be a great way of adding another revenue stream, especially if you aren't in a hurry to see a significant return on your investment.

Scoring on an IPO

Some startups take off to the point where they choose to go public. When a private company goes public, an event known as an Initial Public Offering (IPO) takes place. During an IPO, a fixed share price is set based on the number of outstanding shares and the company's valuation. If you were fortunate enough to get into this company before it took off, chances have you scored shares at a very low price. By the time the company is ready to go public, shares would be worth a lot more.

The way you make money here is by selling your stake once the company has gone public. However, you need to do your homework. Investors who sell right at the opening of the IPO may end up missing out on massive profits. Generally speaking, companies soar in the days following the IPO. In that event, you could make a killing.

However, not all companies soar following their IPO. Some pullback before taking off. So, the safe bet is to sell right at the start of the IPO. This is the most effective way of ensuring a good return. At the end of the day, this is the ultimate buy and hold strategy for private equity.

Cashing in on a Takeover

There are cases in which larger firms take over private companies. When this occurs, shareholders are bought out entirely. In general, the founders retain some interest in the company (it's usually a token gesture), while the rest of shareholders receive their fair share.

Much like an IPO, when a private firm is bought up, it is valued based on its financials and earning potential. This valuation is then divided by the number of outstanding shares. It's at this point where investors clean up. There are cases in which the larger corporation may be willing to pay a premium on top of the share price as a means of getting the deal done.

The Key Is to Get in Early

Most startups do several rounds of financing. In the early going, crowdfunding is one of the easiest ways in which entrepreneurs can raise capital. It can be very hard to attract venture capital firms in the early days. So, smaller investors may find a good opportunity to make a significant investment. Thus, the key to making money in private equity is to get in early.

The caveat here is to make sure you avoid sinking in too much money into a single company. This is important as most companies don't pan out over the long-term. In some cases, you'll get your investment back. In the worst of cases, you'll miss out. Most of the time, you'll make a modest profit.

So, it's important to keep in mind that private equity is about holding your stake for an extended time frame. It might be a matter of years before you see a significant return. But if you happen to hit a home run, it will be worth the while.

There are three things to look at when you plan on investing in private equity:

1. The market for the products and services of the company
2. Sales projections for at least five years
3. The company's track record

If a company fails to produce any of these three items, pass on it. Any company you plan to invest in should at least be able to produce some kind of track record that can back up their claims. Otherwise, investing in an untested company may be nothing more than wishful thinking.

Conclusion

Thank you very much for making it all the way through to the end of this book. The collection of tips, strategies, and techniques in this book have been put together so that you can make the most of your hard-earned money. In particular, making money is not about having a vast capital. It's about playing your cards right.

Now that you have finished this book, the time has come to put these strategies into practice. To begin with, you can choose the most appealing strategy. It doesn't matter which one you choose. The point is to get started somewhere.
Then, sit down and figure out how much you could reasonably set aside for investing in this venture. Depending on the amount you have available, you can start with micro-investing (such as Acorns), or perhaps try something bigger like day trading.

One of the most important aspects to consider is your aims. When you set out to invest, it's important to know the main reason why you are doing so. Regardless of the specific reason, you need to be prepared to be patient. Patience is the key to making significant profits in investing.

Those who are looking for a get-rich-quick proposition, they had better look elsewhere. The fact of the matter is that starting small requires patience. Eventually, investments begin to pay off. But that requires time and dedication. In the long run, the effort is certainly worth it.

Lastly, it's important to focus on building multiple revenue streams. This book has been set up so that you can build several sources of income. When you add them all up, you can finance your lifestyle comfortably. Naturally, the simpler your lifestyle, the easier it will be for you to generate the revenue you need. So, what are you waiting for?

The time has come to make the most of the valuable nuggets of information presented herein. You'll find that once you have mastered the first two or three strategies, the rest will become very easy for you. The most important thing to keep in mind is that you need to start somewhere. The worst thing you can do is keep putting off your investment endeavors.

Ultimately, building a profitable portfolio isn't tough when you know where to put your money. These are the secrets that professional traders and investors learn. Now that you have peered into the world that insiders know, you too have the tools you need to make serious cash.

Thank you once again for taking the time to read this book. If you have found it to be useful and informative, please tell your friends, family, and colleagues about it. They will surely find as much value in it as you have. They'll find that anyone can become a successful investor. This book is the perfect place to start.
Good luck and happy investing!

Description

Have you been looking for a way to supplement your income without having to take on a second job?

Have you been looking for a way to generate additional revenue streams without having to work harder?

Have you been looking for ways you can engage in passive investing without exposing yourself to needless risk?

Have you been looking for ways to earn more money without having to start a new business venture?

If you have answered "yes" to any of these questions, then this is the book for you. In this volume, we will explore investing in the stock market. However, this book is not about the same old ways of investing in stocks. This book is about finding clever ways of making money in financial markets, especially when you don't have much capital to start with.

This book has been written with small investors in mind. These are folks who are willing to put money to work for them but don't have much to start with. In the following chapters, you will learn how you can take small investments, sometimes a little a $1 and turn them into significant returns.

Here is a sample of what you can expect to learn in this book:

- How to make money by using the high-frequency trading strategy
- How to use ETFs to your advantage across various asset classes
- Making money by investing in FOREX
- Using the snowball effect to make a small initial investment grow over time
- The ways in which you can make money by investing in cryptocurrency

- Using precious metals as a means of making money when the stock market is taking a dip
- How to successfully short stocks without exposing yourself to unnecessary risk
- Using options to help you make money without investing much upfront
- The use of a Robo-advisor as a means of automating your investments
- How to make money by investing your spare change

... and much, much more!

If you are looking to get started investing today, but don't have much to start with, this is the book you need to read. Herein, you will find everything you need to know with regard to making money in a simple and effective manner.
Best of all, you will find that don't need money to make money. However, you need to know the tricks of the trade. The information you will find here is usually reserved for insiders. These are the types of secrets that they don't want you to know.

For the first time, you'll be privy to all of these secrets in a straightforward manner. You will find that there are no hidden gimmicks here. Just honest information about how you can turn a small amount of money into a significant return.

This is how the big brokers pad their bonuses.

Now, you, too, can take full advantage of these opportunities. Let's get started on learning how you can make money without having to invest much upfront. Over time, you will build multiple revenue streams and fund your savings.

If that sounds good, then come on in. There's plenty to talk about!

Introduction

An option is basically an agreement on the underlying shares of stock. It's an agreement to exchange shares at a fixed price over a specified timeframe (they can be bought or sold). The first thing that you should understand about options is the following. Why would someone get involved with the options trading in the first place? Most people come to options trading with the hope of earning profits from trading the options themselves. But to truly understand what you're doing, you need to understand why options exist, to begin with.

There are probably three main reasons that options on stocks exist. The first reason is that it allows people that have shares of stock to earn money from their investment in the form of regular income. So, it can be an alternative to dividend income or even enhance dividend income. As we are going to see you later, if you own a minimum of 100 shares of some stock, this is a possibility. Then you can sell options against the stock and earn income from that over time intervals lasting from a week to a month, generally speaking. Obviously, such a move entails some risk, but people will enter positions of that type when the relative risk is low.

The second reason that people get involved with options is that they offer insurance against a collapse of the stock. So, once again, an option involves being able to trade shares of the stock at a fixed price that is set at the time the contract is originated. One type of contract allows the buyer to purchase shares; the other allows the buyer to sell shares. This allows people who own large numbers of shares to purchase something that provides protection of their investment that would allow them to sell the shares at a fixed price, in the event that their stock was declining by vast amounts on the market. So, the concept is exactly like paying insurance premiums. Its unclear how many people actually use this in practice, but this is one of the reasons that options exist. The way this would work would be that you pay someone a premium to secure the right to sell them your stock at a fixed price over some time frame. Then if the share price drops well below that degree to price, you would still be able to sell your shares and avoid huge losses that were occurring on the market.

The third reason that I would give for the existence of options is that it provides a way for people to make arrangements to purchase shares of stock at the prices that they find attractive, which aren't necessarily available on the market. So, there is a degree of speculation here. But let's just say that a particular stock you are interested in is trading at $100 a share. Furthermore, let's assume that people are incredibly bullish on the stock and they are expecting it to rise by a great deal in the coming weeks. Maybe, it's earnings season.

During earnings season, stock can move by massive amounts. But before the earnings call, nobody knows whether the stock is going to go up or down or by how much it's going to move. An options contract could allow someone to speculate and set up a situation where they could profit from a huge move upward without having actually to invest in the stock.

So in that situation, if the stock declined instead, they wouldn't be out of much money. Just for an example, let's say they buy an options contract that allows them to purchase the shares (of the stock currently at $100) for $102, and the option costs two dollars per share. So, the stock would have to go to $104 or higher to make it worth it.

Typically, options contracts involve 100 shares. So, if the speculator bets wrong, the most they would be out would be $200.

Let's just say, after the earnings call, the share price jumps to $120. The speculator can exercise the option, which means they buy the shares at $102 per share. Then they can sell the stock on the market at the price of $120 per share. Taking into account the investment to buy the options contract, that basically leaves them with the sixteen $16 dollars per-share profit. Now, you might say well why didn't they just buy the shares that $100 a share? The reason is if they did that, they would actually be exposed to the stock to the fullest extent possible. Like we said, earnings calls can go both ways. Just recently, Netflix announced that they lost subscribers. In after-hours trading alone, the stock lost $43 per share. So, in our little example, we could say that the stock dropped instead of gaining, let's say to $80 per share. In that case, our speculator would've been in a significant point of pain had they actually purchase the shares ahead of time. By doing the option instead, they set themselves up for profit while only risking a $200 loss. And it turns out that there are strategies you can use with options to profit no matter which way the stock moves. So, I didn't want to get too far ahead of ourselves, but an experienced options trader would have set up a trade designed to earn profits either way.

Types of Options

Options agreements come in two varieties. The first type of options contract is known as a call. A call option gives the buyer the possibility to buy some shares of stock at a fixed price. Usually, it's 100 shares. The agreed-upon value used to trade the shares is called the strike price. Every option comes with an expiration date, and so, if the buyer decides to purchase the shares, they must do so before the option expires. If the buyer decides to buy the shares, they are said to "exercise" the option. The party that sold to open the option, in that case, is said to be "assigned" if someone exercises the contract.

Options can be classified by the way they can be exercised. The possibilities are American-style or European-style. If you can exercise the option on any date, it's known as American style.

If the contract is a European style, the option can only be exercised on the day it expires. It's important to note that these terms don't necessarily mean that the option is trading in Europe or America. Although most options in America are American-style, there are some that are European style. Two examples are SPX and RUT. These are options used to follow the S & P 500 index and the Russell 2000 index. But the vast majority of options you're going to come across are going to be American style. If you sell options, this is something you need to be aware of. That means at any time that the option is an open position for you as a seller, you could be assigned.

The basic rule for a call option is that this is a bullish purchase. If you invest in a call option, your expectation is that's the price of the shares is going to rise. There are two ways that you can take advantage of this. The first way is to trade the option simply. Small moves in the stock price translate into big moves for options prices. So, if the stock goes up in price, you can sell the option and make a profit.

The second way to profit would be actually to exercise the right to buy the shares. In that situation, you would buy the shares for the price per share given by the strike and then sell them on the open market to make a profit. In order to make money, the price on the market must rise to a level more significant than the strike price added to the amount you paid to buy in the position.

So, if you purchased a $50 option for $1, meaning the strike price is $50, the price on the market would have to rise to $51 or higher to make exercising the option profitable.

The rule is that call options increase in price or value primarily when stock prices are rising. But, as we'll see, options are impacted by some other factors as well. But the general bet with a call option is earning profits when the underlying stock goes up in value.

Before we move on to consider the other dominant class of options, we need to make a clear distinction between selling and buying options. We can loosely use this language, but, actually, be applying it in very different contexts. First, let's consider simple options trading which is what most readers are going to be interested in. In this case, you enter a position by purchasing an option. So in market jargon, we would say that you are buying to open. So, in other words, you open your position by purchasing an option. If you buy to open an option you are never at risk of being assigned the shares of stock. So, you can sell the option and that carries no risk to you whatsoever. The only risk that you would face would have to sell the option for a discount compared to what you paid to enter the position.

In contrast, you can also sell to open an options position. When you do that, you are at risk for the assignment with regard to the shares of stock. So that doesn't entail some risk but there are many reasons that people would choose to sell to open an options position. Also, you can sell to open positions in order to earn income from the premium.

The second type of option is called a put. A put option is a contract that allows the buyer to sell shares to the writer of the contract. This would be

100 of stock with a price given by the strike price. So, a put option has a strike price and expiration date just like a call option.

Put options actually increase in value if the market price of the stock declines. So if you buy a put, you are basically shorting the stock. If you intend to exercise the option, it would work in the following way. To use specific numbers, consider an example with the strike price of the option at $100 dollars per share. Then we will suppose that the company had a negative earnings call and the share price drop to $70 a share overnight. If you held the put option, you could buy the shares on the market at $70 a share. Then you can "exercise the option". That means you would sell the shares at the price of $100 a share because that was the strike price on the contract. So, you would make nearly a $30 profit per share by engaging in this trade. The profit would be given by the strike price minus the premium paid to buy the option minus the price you purchase the shares for on the market. So if we just imagine that the option cost $2 a share, the profit, in this case, would be $100 - $2 -$70 = $28 per share. Since there are 100 shares per option contract, that would mean a profit of $2800.

Step-by-step Guide on How to Start Options Trading and Create Passive income

You already know some of the basics that come with working on options as well as some of their benefits. Now it is time to learn how to get started with options so that you can make the money that you want.

But that does not mean that there are no risks involved. Almost every investment entails a multitude of risks. The same goes for options. An investor ought to know of these risks before proceeding with trade.

Options are a part of the group of securities called derivatives. The term derivative is many a time associated with huge risks and volatile performance. Warren Buffett once called derivatives "weapons of mass destruction," which is a little too much.

The term 'derivative' implies that its price is derived from the price of some other object. When it comes to Financial Securities, their derivatives are Options, whose value depends on the price of another asset.

One can gain a real advantage in the market if they know how options work and can use them properly since you can put the cards in your favor if you can use options correctly. The great thing about options is that you can use them according to your style. If you're a speculative person, earn through speculation. If not, earn without speculating. You should know how options work even if you decide never to use them because other companies you invest in might use options. A lot of MNCs use options in many ways. Some companies may give employees potential stock ownership as stock options or use options to hedge foreign-exchange risk.

Getting it all started

You may be excited to jump into the market and start trading right away, but there are a few things that you will need to do first. You will need to start out with a good understanding of the basics that come with options and you need to know some of the option types that you can pick from. We talked about these topics a little bit before, but the more that you can learn about them before investing, the more success you will have.

After you have had some time to understand what options are all about and what you will be getting yourself into, it is time to come up with your motivation for trading. Ask yourself how much money you are looking to make from this trade and how you would like to use that money when you have earned it. This motivation is going to help you out so much when you are in the thick of the trading and you need some help staying focus.

But one of the most important things that you will need to focus on when you first get started is having what is called a trading plan. The trading plan is going to basically list all of the things that you want to be able to accomplish while you are trading. It can include what you expect to happen, some of your goals, the strategy that you will go with, and any other guidelines that will help you be successful. Those who decide to start investing in options without having a good plan in place will be the ones who run into a lot of risks.

Determine whether you will proceed as a company or an individual

Both these alternatives are a lot different when actual options trading come into practice. The legal obligations of both vary significantly. Besides, check whether you're allowed to trade with an offshore company or an offshore bank account. This could be advantageous in some tax-related situations. Non-resident citizen offshore companies and bank accounts are quite beneficial.

Get a trading account

Setting up an online trading account is the foremost thing to do when starting trading in options. Step by step instructions is provided by companies, which makes it very easy to manage the account. But this process does take some time, so start early.

A lot of factors are taken into consideration while deciding on your trading account.

The amount of money you're planning to invest in is the first thing that defines the type of account, which will be opened.

A very modest amount of start-up money is required to start trading in stock only. Even 200$ will work. But a Basic options account requires a minimum start-up of 2000$. If you have enough capital, setting up a day-trading account shall be an optimal choice. This account enables you to buy and sell as many times as you want.

Another choice one may get is if they want to open a margin account or not. A Margin account has its benefits.

After selling a stock or option, you get the money immediately, which in turn enables you to buy again. Some time is required in a regular account to clear the proceeds from a sale. A Margin Account enables you to borrow money to trade while using your own capital at the same time. One can say that it is similar to an overdraft facility, which allows you to get extra funds.

There's a catch though. A margin account requires a lot of time to be approved. You can start with a regular account and apply for a margin account later. You must use your own money in a regular account and setting it up is less time-consuming.

The need for research companies and their relevance

Acquiring the best research information can be a tedious task. The market has a lot of research groups. To make successful trades and make your ventures profitable, up to date information about options is of utmost importance. One needs to be completely aware of the existing market conditions. So, you can look for companies that provide this information and make more informed decisions.

Select a Security

This can be done by researching the finance sections of major news corporations. A simple search will turn up results such as CNN's Money section, which lists the most active companies according to the S&P 500. If the investor is already partially immersed in the finance world, it would be wise to seek out the advice of a friend or mentor. New options traders, and particularly those who are new to trading in general, should approach options trading cautiously. Rather than diving right in, investors should get their feet wet by experimenting with a limited number of securities and options so that they can keep track of gains and losses and avoid mistakes for future investments.

Choose OTC or Regulated Trading

While this can be decided at a later stage, it is suggested here so that new investors can refer to the boards of a regulated exchange, such as the New York Stock Exchange, when choosing a put or call that is well suited to their tastes. Practiced traders can pick up an OTC option later if desired, such as a call to cover the cost of an insurance put, also known as a married put.

Select Strategies

Before beginning trading, investors will need to be sure they are familiar with a few simple strategies that can be implemented with a stock.

Examine the Market

Investors will need to study the time frame charts associated with their underlying security selection. Take into account all three trends in regard to the time frame and note how the security is moving within each.

Purchase Options and Trade

Finally, the moment investors have been waiting for. Based upon conclusions drawn from studying time frame charts, investors will need to buy the appropriate calls or puts. At the same time, investors should choose one or two of the strategies with which they are already familiar that they believe will work well in the present market climate. If trading via a regulated exchange, options for the strategies may be selected from a list published by the exchange.

Getting a broker

Interactive Brokers are favorable in case you open only one account. They offer quick options information while being less expensive than other alternatives.

A lot of online brokers can be found, but they charge a certain amount for their services, which can affect your profit margin in the initial stages of trading.

The broker is going to be the person who works with you and often will be able to give you advice and help you to make the trades that you want. All brokers that you go with will require some fees or a commission that you will need to pay to use their services, so you must factor this in when figuring out the costs that you want to incur. There are many different types of brokers that you are able to go with and the price that you pay will depend on the type and amount of services you choose to go with.

When you pick out the broker you want to work with, you will probably need to meet with them in the beginning and discuss your trading plan and how they will be able to help. They will go over a risk assessment with you, so they know where you stand with the amount of risks that you are willing to take. It is a good place for you and the broker to get started together so you are on the same page and are able to get things done.

Appreciate That Options Trading Is Not Simple

It is vital at this stage to recapitulate the meaning of options trading. This is a contract that grants one the right of either buying or selling a security based on the speculative value of it in a limited period of time. However, the contract is not obligatory in nature. In understanding options trading, two forms of it have to be understood; first is a call option, and the other is the put option. The two are opposites of each other. One buys the former option when one expects an asset's value to go up over time but before the deadline of expiry of the contract expires.

However, participating in this market requires one to have enough understanding of how it works. Any venture requires one to learn enough. Educating oneself generally about investment is the best standing point. This creates understanding and ensures that one is able to comprehend the way that the options trading market as an investment venture works.

Among the reasons why people should educate themselves on options trading is because it does not work in certain ways. It also does not have guarantees of profit. This means that it, just like other ventures, involves risks that should be understood. The risks in the case of trading options are quite extreme. It requires calculation and being accurate as one speculates about the drop and rising of the value of the options on offer. Being interest in a venture that involves a high-risk level requires enough knowledge and sometimes mentorship by those who have prior knowledge and understanding of the market in order to avoid plunging into frustration and wastage of capital.

The Options Trader Mindset

Options trading are not something that is for everyone. Options trading are most suitable for a certain personality type and mindset. But if you are intrigued by the concept of options, but you simply have not had a chance to develop the correct mindset before, there are a few tips that we can rely on in order to get in the right frame of mind.

You are able to weather the storm

Options prices can move a lot over the course of short time periods. So someone who likes to see their money protected and not losing any is not going to be suitable for options trading. Now, we all want to come out ahead, so I am not saying that you have to be happy about losing money in order to be an options trader. What you have to be willing to do is calmly observe your options losing money, and then be ready to stick it out in order to see gains return in the future. This is akin to riding a real roller coaster, but it is a financial roller coaster. Options do not slowly appreciate the way a Warren Buffett investor would hope to see. Options move big on a percentage basis, and they move fast. If you are trading multiple contracts at once, you might see yourself losing $500 and then earning $500 over a matter of a few hours. In this sense, although most options traders are not "day traders" technically speaking, you will be better off if you have a little bit of a day trading mindset.

You don't make emotional decisions

Since options are, by their nature, volatile, and very volatile for many stocks, coming to options trading and being really emotional about it is not a good way to approach your trading. If you are emotional, you are going to exit your trades at the wrong time in 75% of cases. You don't want to make any sudden moves when it comes to trading options. As we have said, you should have a trading plan with rules on exiting your positions, stick to those rules and you should be fine.

Be a little bit math-oriented

In order to really understand options trading and be successful, you cannot be shy about numbers. Options trading are a numbers game. That doesn't mean you have to drive over to the nearest university and get a statistics degree. But if you do understand probability and statistics, you are going to be a better options trader. Frankly, it's hard to see how you can be a good options trader without having a mind for numbers. Some math is at the core of options trading and you cannot get around it.

You are market-focused

You don't have to set up a day trading office with ten computer screens so you can be tracking everything by the moment, but if you are hoping to set up a trade and lazily come back to check it three days later, that isn't going to work with options trading. You do need to be checking your trades a few times a day. You also need to be keeping up with the latest financial and economic news, and you need to keep up with any news directly related to the companies you invest in or any news that could impact those companies. If the news does come out, you are going to need to make decisions if it's news that isn't going to be favorable to your positions. Also, you need to be checking the charts periodically so you have an idea of where things are heading for now.

Focus on a trading style

As you can see, there are many different ways that you can trade options. In my opinion, sticking to one or two strategies is the best way to approach options trading. I started off buying call options, but now, I focus on selling put credit spreads and iron condors. You should pick what you like best and also something that aligns with your goals. I moved into selling put credit spreads and iron condors because I became interested in the idea of making a living from options trading with regular income payments, rather than continuing to buy calls and hope that the share price would go up. There is no right or wrong answer, pick the trading style that is best suited to your own personal style and needs.

Keep detailed trading journals

It's easy to fool yourself when trading options, especially if you are a beginner. I hate to make the analogy, but this is kind of like going to the casino. If you have friends that gamble at casinos, then you are going to notice that they tend to remember the wins, and they will forget all the times that they gambled and lost. I had a cousin that won a boat, and she was always bragging about how she won a boat at the casino. I remember telling her that yes she won a boat, but she paid $65,000 more than the boat was worth to the casino over the years. You don't want to get in the same situation with your options trading. It can be an emotional experience because trading options is active and fast-paced. When you have a profitable trade, it will be exciting. But you need to keep a journal to record all of your trades, in order to know exactly what the real situation is. That doesn't mean you quit if you look at your journal and find out you have a losing record, what you do is figure out why your trades aren't profitable and then make adjustments.

Options traders are flexible

I have said this before, but one thing you need to remember about options trading is you can make money no matter what happens to the stock. So you need to avoid falling into the trap of only trading options to make money one way. Most frequently, people do what they have been brainwashed to do and they will trade call options hoping to profit from rising share prices. If you are in that mindset now, you need to challenge yourself and begin trading in different ways, so you can actually experience making money from declining stock prices, or in the case of iron condors, stock prices that don't even change at all. You need to be able to adapt to changing market conditions in order to profit as an options trader. So don't entrap yourself by only using one method. Earlier, I said to use one or two styles, but you should be ready to branch out when market conditions change. Remember this – market conditions always change eventually. As I am writing, this we are in the midst of a long-term bull market, but it won't last forever.

Take a disciplined approach

Don't just buy options for a certain stock because it feels good. You need to do research on your stocks. That will include doing fundamental analysis. This is going to mean paying attention to the history of a stock, knowing what the typical ranges are for, stock in recent history is, and also reading through the company's financial statements and prospectus. Remember, I suggest picking three companies to trade options on for a year and also two index funds. The index funds require less research, but for the three companies that you pick, you should get to know those companies inside and out. Stick with them for a year, at the end of each year, evaluates each company. Then decide if you want to keep them and bring them forward into the following year's trades. If one company is not working out for you, then move on and try a different company.

Puts and Calls

Put and call options are referred to as a derivative investment. The movements of their prices depend on the movements of prices of a different financial product, also referred to as the underlying.

So, what is an option? It is defined as the right to sell or buy a certain stock with a set price given a specific time frame. With options, you won't have outright ownership of the shares, but you make calculated bets on a stock's price and what its value will be in the future, given the specified expiration of the option. What makes options attractive is that you are to choose whether you want to exercise them or not. If your bet is wrong, you can let the options expire. Although the options' original cost is lost, it still wouldn't compare had you paid for the stock's full price.

Call options are purchased when the trader is expecting the underlying's price to go up within a particular time frame.

Put options are purchased when the trader is expecting the underlying's price to go down within a particular time frame.

There's an option for puts and calls to be written or sold. This will still generate income, but certain rights have to be given up to the option's buyer.

For options defined for the US, a call is defined as an options contract giving the buyer rights to buy an underlying asset at a previously set price any time until the expiration date. For options defined for the EU, buyers can choose to exercise the option to purchase the underlying but only on the set expiration date.

The strike price is defined as a price previously determined at which the call buyer has the choice to purchase the underlying asset. For example, a buyer of a certain stock calls option with a 10$ strike price may opt to purchase that stock at the same price before the expiration date of the option.

The expiration of options may vary. It can also be short or long term. It can be worth the while for call buyers to exercise the option, which is to require the writer or seller of the call to sell the stocks at the set strike price., but only if the underlying's current price is more than the strike price. For example, if a stock trades at $10 at the stock market, it is not profitable for the buyer of the call option to exercise the choice to purchase that stock at $11 since they could get the same on the market at a lower price.

Put buyers reserve the right to sell stocks at strike price during a set time range.

The highs and lows the stock market goes through can be both exciting and nerve-wracking for newbie or veteran investors. Risking hard-earned money can make anyone anxious. But played right with sound and well-planned strategies, you can be successful in this field

If you are looking for a way to invest in the stock market but you are trying to avoid the risk of directly selling stocks or buying them, options trading might be perfect for you. Options are typically traded at significantly lower prices compared to the underlying prices of the actual shares. This makes trading them a less risky way to control a large stock position, although you don't own the shares. Using options strategically allows risk mitigation while maintaining huge profit potentials and you will be playing in the field even if you're investing just a fraction of the stock's price.

All of these benefits of options trading got you excited, right? After all, options have a lower risk and they're a lot cheaper. There are two major disadvantages, however – the limited-time aspect and the reality that you don't own the stock until you choose to exercise your options.

Call Options

With call options, what you pay for is just 'rights to buy' certain shares at a set price and covered by a specific time frame. Let's say that stock ABC is selling for $90 per share in May. If you believe that the stock's price will go up over a few months, you'd purchase a three-month option to buy 100 shares of ABC by August 31 for $100. For this sample call option, you would be paying around $200 if the option cost per share is $2. In options, you are only allowed to buy in increments of 100 shares. This gives you the choice to purchase 100 shares of ABC anytime within the three-month timeframe. The $200 investment is significantly lower than the $9,000 you would have had to shell out if you bought 1000 shares outright.

If you bet right and on July 15, if the ABC shares hit the market at $115, you may exercise the call option and you would have gained $1,300 (that's 100 shares multiplied by the $15 profit you gained per share and deducted by your original investment of $200). If you don't have the resources to buy the shares, you can also make a profit if you re-sell the option to another investor or via the open market. The gain will be pretty much similar to this option.

If you bet wrong, and the price of ABC's shares fell to $80 never to reach $100 within the three-month timeframe, you can let the option reach its expiration, which saves you money (if you bought the shares outright, your original investment of $9,000 is now down to a value of only $8,000, so you lost $1000). This means you only lost $200, which was your investment for the call option.

Risks Involved in Call Options

Like any other form of investment, options have their share of potential risks. Taking the second scenario where you bet wrong as an example and stock ABC never got to $100 during the option's timeframe of three months, you would have lost the entire $200 of your investment, right? In terms of loss percentage, that's %100. Anyone who's been playing the stock market would tell you that it's extremely rare for an investor to suffer a 100% loss. This scenario can only happen if ABC suddenly went bankrupt, causing the price of their stocks to plummet down to zero value.

Therefore, if you look at it from a point of view of percentages, options can cause you huge losses. Let's elaborate on this point. If the price of ABC's share went up to $99 and it's the last day for you to exercise the option, choosing to purchase the shares will mean losing a dollar for each share. What if you invested $9,000 for the stock and you owned 100 stock shares. In three months, which is the option's expiration date if you took it, you would have gained 10% from your original investment ($99 from $90). Comparing both, you would have gained 10% if you purchased the shares outright and lost %100 if you chose the option but did not exercise it. This example shows how risky options can be.

However, the opposite can happen if stock ABC reached a price higher than $100. If you purchased the option, your gain percentage would have been substantially higher compared to buying the stocks outright. If the stock reached $110, you would have gained 400% ($10 gain versus the $2 per share investment) if you went for the option and only gained 22%

($20 gain versus the $90 per share investment) if you purchased the shares.

Lastly, when you own the stock, nothing can force you to sell. That means if after three months, and stock ABC's price goes down, you can hang on to it if you believe it still has the potential to recover and even increase in value compared to the original. If the price goes up dramatically, you'll make significant gains and you didn't incur losses. However, if you chose options as your investment method, the expiration would have forced you to suffer a 100% loss after the set timeframe. There will be no option to hold on to the stock even if you believe it will go up in value soon.

Options have major pros and also major cons. You need to be aware of these before you step into the arena of options trading.

Put Options

On the other side of the options investment is the put option. Whereas call is the right to purchase, 'put' gives you the option to sell a certain security at a set price within a specific time frame. Investors usually purchase put options to protect the price of a stock in case it suddenly drops down, or even the market itself. With put options, you can sell the shares and your investment portfolio is protected from unexpected market swings. Put options are, therefore, a way to hedge your portfolio or lower its risk.

For example, you have invested in stock ABC for 100 shares, which you bought for $50 per share. As of May 31, the price per share has reached a market high $70. Of course, you'd want to maintain this position in your stock, and at the same time protect your gained profits in case the price of this stock goes down. To fit your requirements, you may purchase a put option with a three-month expiration and $70 per share strike price.

If ABC's stock price goes down drastically over the next couple of months, reaching a low per-share price of only $60, you will still be protected. By exercising your put option, you will still be able to sell the shares at $70 each even if stock ABC is now trading at a lower value. If you are feeling confident that ABC can still recover in the future, you can hold on to the stock and just resell the put option. The price of this put option will have gone up because of the diving stock ABC took.

On the other hand, if stock ABC's value kept climbing, just let the put option expire and you would still profit from the increased price of the shares. Even though you lost what you have invested in the put option, you still have the underlying stock with you. Therefore, you can view the put option as a kind of insurance policy for your investment, which may or may not use. Another thing to remember is that you can purchase put options even if you don't own the underlying stock, just like you would in a call option. You are not required to own the stock itself.

Risks Involved in Put Options

Just as with call options, put options carry the same risks. There is also a 100% loss potential when the underlying stock price goes up, and a huge gain when the price dives because you can resell the option for a higher price.

Options Trading Simulator

There is a close link between stock trading and options trading. However, options are not the same as stocks. Options are largely used to generate a profit using much smaller investments compared to stock investments. Another use of options is to insure against losses.

There are quite a number of reputable simulators online and one of the most reliable and trusted one is the simulator from Investopedia. This firm is not only the leading financial information and services firm but has an amazing wealth of resources online. The simulator uses actual data from stock markets so as to produce real life experience of using a real brokerage account.

Introduction to the trade simulator

The trade simulator is used for a number of reasons by different people. For instance, instructors use it as an instrument to teach their students all about the stock and options markets and how to use it. Some people use this simulator to try out new trading strategies while others just use it to find out what the real trading account feels like. Basically, the main purpose of the simulator is to make you simply, or any other user, a better trader.

There are a couple of tabs located on the top side of the user interface. When you click any of these tabs, then more links will appear and these will offer you more choices. Here is a look at the 7 separate tabs found on the online trading simulator.

Tabs on the trading simulator

Home: The home button takes you to the home page and gives you an overall outlook of your trading account. Here, you are able to access other tabs and get to the pages you desire. At the home page, you also get an opportunity to change your settings and profile.

Portfolio tab: This particular tab provides users with a summary of the stocks, shares, options and all other holdings.

Watch list tab: This particular tab enables you to easily and efficiently track any stocks you want but without allocating any cash to any part of the portfolio. It is easy to add new stocks and manage the current ones from here.

Stock research: The stock research tab comes with important tools that enable users to carry out research on the performance of stocks and of companies that they may be interested in. Some of the tools available include a ticker lookup tool, a research tool and so much more.

The trading tab: This tab contains the simulator where users get to enter or input their trade orders. They are also able to review all open, failed and outstanding trades.

Ranking tab: Another tab you will notice on the options trading tab is the ranking tab. This is an important tab that instantly lets you know of your current placing enabling you to opt for any specific competition.

Messages tab: This is a tab that allows users to check your messages that are in your inbox. There will sometimes be messages sent to you and users will also be able to send messages to others.

Games tab: There is a games tab on the trade simulator that allows any user to manage, review and create games. You will find active games which you can join and participate in. users are by default invited to join in some games and the choice to join in or not is voluntarily made.

Awards: Any user who successfully completes different trade simulator activities, especially trade activities gets to receive an award.

Help: It is always good to know that help is at hand whenever needed. As a trader and investor, if you ever need help with tutorials or have any general questions, then you simply need to click this tab.

Using the simulator to place orders and buy stock options

You are now familiar with the tabs on the trade simulator and can use these buttons at any stage of trade. The next step now is to set up and submit a trade using this simulator. We will now endeavor to purchase 100 shares of Walmart Stores Inc., abbreviated as WMT.

First, choose the trade tab and then enter WMT and 100. Figure 100 is entered in the quantity field while WMT is entered in the symbol field. The transaction needed is "Buy" while the price selected is market. The simulator will require a duration period and here you choose "Good Till Canceled".

Now select the Preview Order so as to view the order confirmation. The Preview Order will show the stock purchased, the type of trade, price and many other essential details that you need to trade successfully.

Please take a minute and confirm each and every detail on this preview. Ensure that all the details match what your trade details are. This is indeed a confirmation process, that you are buying 100 shares of Walmart Stores, abbreviated WMT at market rates. For a real trade online, you would be charged a commission fee of about $20. Brokerage firms will charge you a commission for executing the trades on your behalf.

As soon as you confirm all the details on the Preview Page are, you may then proceed to submit the page. This will confirm your purchase of 100 shares of WMT at current market price. The order will now be filled when the next available opportunity presents itself. Should an order be placed outside of regular working hours, then the order will be executed first thing on the next trading day. Your order can be confirmed by checking out the order submission page. The stock simulator will confirm this for you.

The simulator will also indicate the stocks with the biggest gains on that particular day and those with the biggest losses. This is important information that can help and guide traders on how to place their trades.

If you check out your portfolio page, it should now indicate 100 shares of WMT as well as some cash balance. Now here is what the various items on the portfolio page mean.

Buying power: This refers to your capacity to buy options or shares and to trade. The buying power is typically based on your portfolio's value as well as cash amount. It is not possible to make trades that do exceed your indicated buying power.

Account value: This value means the total value of the portfolio as of that particular moment. This value is updated each night once the markets close. The currency of the account is also indicated in brackets.

Annual return: This term on your purchase page refers to the total returns, as a percentage, if all your annual returns were to be extrapolated for a given year.

Cash: Here, the amount of cash that you have in your account at the given moment will be displayed. The buying power display is considered a better indicator of financial position.

You will note that the account on the simulator is divided into 3 distinct parts. These are the option portfolio, the stock portfolio, and the shorted stock portfolio. The stock portfolio will indicate all the stocks that you currently have. It will indicate all the different values such as company name, the number of shares and so on.

It is important to learn how to interpret the Portfolio Summary page, it is important to now apply all these tools and ensure that you conduct trades as required. Let us now learn something else on the simulator.

Use of ticker symbol on the simulator

Even as you purchase stocks and options on the simulator, you may have noticed the system requesting a company's stock symbol in order to place a trade. Each company that joins the markets receives a unique stock symbol. Once the symbol is awarded, it will be unique to the company and none other can use this symbol.

The ticker symbol is sometimes chosen by the company itself or the bourse. It can be as brief as one single letter or as long as 5 letters. For instance, Ford Motor Company uses the letter F as its symbol

Ticker symbols

In many instances, news reports often quote companies using their initials which may confuse others to think of the initials as the ticker symbol. For instance, many newspapers across America often refer to the company Hewlett Packard as HP yet the company is quoted on the bourse as HPQ. This shows the need and importance of confirming a company's denotation or ticker symbol before entering any trades.

Any time you wish to purchase shares, stocks or options and all other financial instruments quoted at the markets, make sure to check the ticker symbol. Do not make a guess or an assumption otherwise you may purchase the wrong stock. Fortunately, most brokerage firms allow you to look up ticker symbols with their accounts. The trade simulator provides the same tool to search for a company's ticker symbol.

How to research ticker symbols on the simulator

Now, try and search for the ticker symbols of companies such as Pier 1 Imports and Nike. First, you click on the symbol lookup tab. This tab is found when you click on the Stock Research tab. You will receive a prompt so proceed and enter the search term, Nike and click search or enter. You will be shown the symbol NKE and a confirmation of the company whose ticker this is.

Similarly, when you follow the same procedure to find the ticker symbol of Pier 1 Imports, then you will receive the ticker symbol PIR and a confirmation of the company's details. This shows how fast and easy it is to find a company's ticker symbol.

Diversify your portfolio with the simulator

As an investor and trader, you should always diversify your portfolio. If you do not and instead put all your funds in a single product, then you risk losing all your funds should things not work out with the trade. Simply put, you should always diversify your trades.

The best way to succeed is to purchase and build a diversified equity portfolio. However, you need to be smart when you diversify. For instance, if you choose to invest in McDonald's Corporation, you should avoid investing in another fast food chain.

The reason is that, if the fast food industry were affected, your investments as a whole would take a hit. You should, therefore, buy some

McDonald's shares and then diversify into a different field, say energy sector. You can consider buying shares in ExxonMobil, for instance.

When making real life decisions, you need to take a more scientific approach. This means using a system that ensures you diversify your portfolio in the right manner.

The GICS or Global Industry Classification Standards is widely used by traders, investors and fund managers among many others to diversify their portfolios. This system splits the economy into 10 different sectors. These 1o sectors are listed below.

1. Energy

2. Financials

3. Materials

5. Industrials

6. Utilities

7. Information Technology

8. Telecoms

9. Consumer

10. Health Care

Let us assume you already own WMT, PIR and TLAB shares. This means you own shares of Walmart, Pier 1 Imports, and Tellabs. You, therefore, want to avoid buying shares or stocks in the Telecom or consumer discretionary sectors. However, you can still purchase stock from 8 sectors. With the simulator, you can use a stock screener to get a list of available stocks within a particular sector.

Simply get onto the simulator and run a stock screen for your preferred sector. Now proceed to check out which stocks meet your analysis requirements and also interest you. There is a lot more to portfolio diversification and all these cannot be summarized here. Traders and investors often consider many other factors when diversifying their investments.

Strategies of Trading Options

If you set up with a dealer, and you've got your very own trading room ready to go, a successful plan would be needed. Day-trading techniques come in all shapes and sizes, some simple and others complex. Before we look at an example, there are a few critical components that will involve most techniques. When you transact using the internet, you can typically use charts and trends to forecast potential changes in prices. They are based on fundamental theory, that history is repeating itself, and you will find many a wealthy trader who wholeheartedly agrees with that assertion.

Your map will claim the latest selling options indicators. These vary from strategy to strategy, which includes the Put-Call Ratio Tracker Capital Flow Index Open Interest Relative Strength Index Bollinger Bands. You'll find that it takes hard work and experience to exchange trends for options. You would need to smooth out any creases and try several different charts before you find one with numbers that paints a good picture.

1. Covered Call Options

A call option is a contract option in which the holder (buyer) has the right (but not the obligation) to purchase a defined volume of a commodity at a predetermined date (strike price) within a given time (until its expiry).

This constitutes a duty for the writer (seller) of a call option to sell the underlying security at strike price if the option is exercised. A prime is paid to the call choice writer for taking on the risk involved with the responsibility.

Each deal includes 100 shares, with stock options. The short call is protected if the writer of the call option owns the required amount of the security underlying it. The covered call is a common option technique that helps the stockholder to produce additional income from their stock holdings by periodic call options sales. For more info, please see our covered call strategy post. Someone should buy a bull call spread as an alternative to writing covered calls with a comparable benefit opportunity but with considerably less capital need. Instead of buying the underlying shares of the covered call strategy, the preferred bull call spread approach requires only that the trader purchase deep-in-the-money call options.

Because the aim of writing protected calls is to collect premiums, it makes sense to sell near-month options when time decay on those options is at its highest. Hence, the two tactics we equate would include selling marginally out-of-the-money call options in the near-month timeframe.

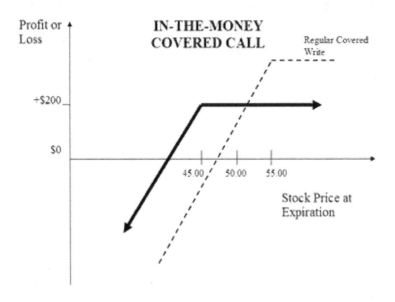

2. Married Put Options

Both married put and long call have the same infinite benefit potential with no cap onto the underlying stock price appreciation. However, benefit is often lower than just owning the stock, lowered by the cost or premium of the purchased option. Reaching break-even for strategy happens when the underlying stock increases by the amount of premium options received. Anything beyond that is income.

The advantage of a married put is that the stock now has a floor minimizing downside risk. The floor is the difference between the underlying stock price, when the put was bought, and the put strike price. Simply put, when the option was acquired, if the underlying stock sold precisely at the strike price, the strategy loss is capped at exactly the price paid for the opportunity.

A married put is also called a long synthetic call, as it has the same profile. The strategy resembles purchasing a standard call option (without the underlying stock) because for both, the same dynamic is real: limited risk, infinite profit potential. The difference between these approaches is clearly how much less money a long call takes.

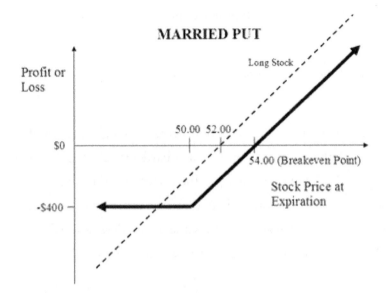

MARRIED PUT

Profit or Loss

Long Stock

50.00 52.00

$0

54.00 (Breakeven Point)

Stock Price at Expiration

-$400

3. Bull Call Spread Options

One may buy a bull call spread as an alternative to writing covered calls with a comparable benefit opportunity but with considerably less capital need. Because of purchasing the underlying stock of the covered call strategy, the preferred bull call spread approach requires only that the trader buy deep-in-the-money call options.

If the aim of writing protected calls is to collect premiums, it makes sense to sell near-month options when time decay for those options is at its highest. Hence, the two tactics we equate would include selling marginally out-of-the-money call options in the near-month period. The distribution of the bull call reduces the call option's risk, but it comes at a trade-off. The stock market returns are also capped, thereby having a small spectrum where the buyer will make a return. Traders will use the spread of the bull call as they expect the valuation of a commodity should increase moderately. Quite likely, they'll use this technique at periods of high uncertainty.

The distribution of the bull call consists of steps which require two call options.

Pick the investments that you believe would grow over a given span of days, weeks, or months. Buy a call option on a particular closing date at a strike price above the selling rate, and pay the premium. With this alternative, another name is a long call. Around the same time, sell a call option at a higher strike price and has the same expiry date as the first call option. Another term for a quick call for this alternative is.

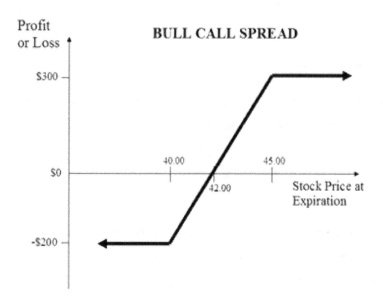

4. Bear Put Spread Options

A bear put spread is a form of options strategy where an investor or trader expects a moderate downturn in security or asset prices. Bear put propagation is accomplished by purchasing put options when selling the same number of puts on the same security at the same expiry date at a lower strike price. With this method, the potential profit is the difference between the two strike costs, minus the options' net value.

For a note, an option is a right to sell a given quantity of underlying security at a defined strike price.

Often known as a debit put spread or a long put spread. A bear put spread is an options technique executed by a bearish trader who aims to increase income while reducing profits.

A bear put spread approach entails purchasing and selling puts on the same underlying asset at the same expiry date but at different strike rates.

A bear puts spread net profit as the price of the underlying security decreases. Therefore, net capital outlay is smaller than buying a single put outright. It also carries much less risk than shortening stock or protection, as the risk is limited to bear put spread net expense. Theoretically, selling a stock short has infinite chance if price goes higher. Unless the investor assumes the underlying stock or asset would decline by a small sum between the day of settlement and the expiry date, a bear put spread may be a perfect strategy. But, if the underlying stock or security declines by more than the dealer gives up the right to demand the extra Benefit. The trade-off between risk and future gain draws many traders.

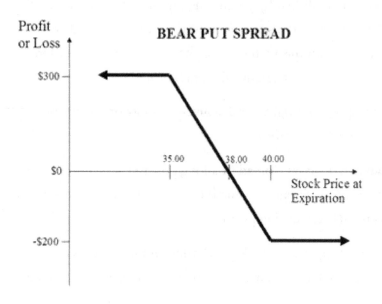

Profit or Loss

BEAR PUT SPREAD

$300

35.00   38.00   40.00

$0

Stock Price at
Expiration

-$200

5. Protective Collar Options

The protective collar technique is where you purchase some protection options, sell a short call option and purchase a long-placed option to reduce downside risk. This technique defends stocks from low market values. It uses cash-on-call options when sold and a Put option when purchased.

Everyone else holds short securities, and the lender must pay the responsibility. Long Put Option is purchasing shares, assuming the stock price should be smaller than the expiry strike price. The investor holds the shares.

Fast call option – selling the current call option until the investor feels market price would sink below the call strike point. The holder will benefit. Although the buyer will not own these shares, they must purchase them again later as the price falls and pay the owner.

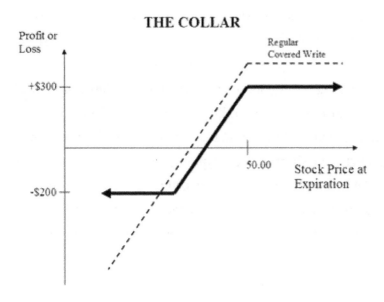

THE COLLAR

Profit or Loss

Regular Covered Write

+$300

50.00

Stock Price at Expiration

-$200

6. Long and Short Strangle Options

The endless options strangle a tremendous benefit, minimal risk approach that is taken while the dealer of the options considers the underlying stock and expiry date. Significant returns are obtained with the long strangle option strategy when the underlying stock price takes a very considerable step either upward or downward at expiry. The formula for estimating profit is given below:

Maximum Benefit = Unlimited Benefit Gained When Underlying Price > Long Call Strike Price + Net Premium Paid OR Underlying Price < Long Put Strike Price — Net Premium Paid Income = Underlying Price — Long Call Strike Price — Net Premium Paid OR Long Put Strike Price — Underlying Price — Net Premium Paid

A medium strangles one quick call with a higher trigger price and one low shot. All options have the same underlying supply and expiry date but different strike rates. If the underlying stock trades in a narrow range below the break-even points, a short strangle is formed for a net credit (or net receipt). Benefit opportunity is limited to cumulative contributions earning fewer commissions. Potential liability is infinite if stock demand increases, and asset selling declines significantly. Full benefit efficiency is limited to overall fewer commissions earned. Total Benefit is gained if the short strangle expires, the stock price trades at or below strike rates, and all options expire worthlessly. The maximum probability of profit loss is infinite because the stock price can grow forever. The potential risk is significant on the downside when the stock price can fall to zero.

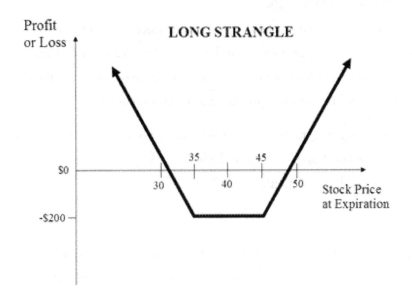

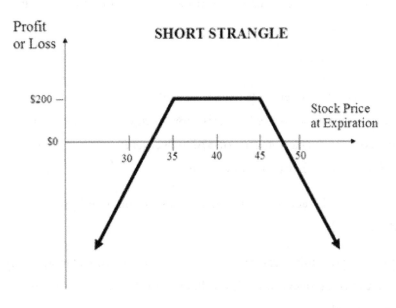

Financial Leverage

Leverage is a concept that is used by both companies and investors. For investors, the notion of leverage is used to try and increase returns that come on investment. To use leverage, you have to make use of various instruments, including future, options, and margin accounts.

The use of leverage n options trading helps boost your profits. Trading in options can give you huge leverage and allow you to generate huge profits from a small investment.

Definition

Leverage is the ability to trade a large number of options using just a small amount of capital. Many traders feel that leverage is, but studies have found that the risk in leveraged options is nearly the same to non-leveraged securities.

Why Is Leverage Riskier?

Trading options using leverage is usually considered riskier because it exaggerates the potential of the business. For instance, you can use $500 to enter a trade that has a potential of $7000. Remember the first rule of trading – don't trade what you cannot lose.

This isn't as true as it seems which is why it is vital that you know what you are doing at all times.

Leverage makes you utilize capital more efficiently. For this reason, many traders love the trade because it allows them to go for larger positions with limited capital.

When you use leverage, you don't reduce the potential profit that you will gain; rather, you reduce the risk in certain trades. For instance, if you want to put your money in 10,000 options at $8 per share, you would need to risk $80,000 worth of investment. This means that the whole amount of $80,000 would be at risk. However, you can use leverage to place a smaller amount of money, thus reducing the risk of loss.

This is the way you need to look at leverage, which is the right way.

Before you can trade leverage, you need to find a way to maximize the gains in each trade. Here are a few tips that you can explore:

Know When to Run

You need to cut losses early enough and then let your winning trades run to completion. Just the way you run other trades; you need to know when to cut your losses so that you don't end up bankrupt. You need to make use of stop losses when running leverage in trades.

Have a Stop Loss Set

As a trader, you need to determine your stop loss set so that you don't lose more than you can afford. The set that you come up with will depend upon the situation of the market at any time. Whatever the case, always make sure you have a set to guide you.

Don't Go With the Trade

Many traders try to chase a trade to the finish, something that ends up discouraging them and making them lose money. Once a move happens, you need to accept and wait for the next opening. Always be patient because just like the other opportunity came along, another one will definitely come by.

Have Limit Orders

Instead of placing market limits, opt for limit orders instead so that you can save on fees. The limit orders also help you reign in your emotions when you trade.

Learn About Technical Analysis

Make sure you learn about technical analysis before you jump into trading. Technical analysis will make sure you have the information that you need to make decisions fast.

The Advantages of Leverage in Options Trading

When you use leverage, you increase your financial capability as a trader and enjoy better trading results. You can change the amount of leverage at your discretion. This is because when you open a trading account, you have all the power of managing the amount of capital that you place on a trade. The good news is that you can use leverage free of charge, but you need to make sure you know how it works and whether it will work for you or not.

The level of leverage varies. Some trading platforms offer leverage from as low as 1:1 up to and beyond 1:1000. As a trader, it is advisable that you go for the largest leverage possible so that you can make the biggest returns.

Another advantage is that low leverage allows you as a new trader to survive. When starting out in options trading, you have the capacity to make small trades with little to show for your efforts. With leverage, you can make use of leverage to place trades that run into thousands of dollars without risking the same amount in terms of investment. As long as you know what you are doing, you have the capability to enjoy massive profits.

Disadvantages of Leverage in Options Trading

As much as it is a good way to make huge profits, you also need to understand that leverage comes with many demerits. These include:

Magnifies the Losses

With leverage, you will be faced with huge losses if the trade decides to go the other way. And since the original outlay is way smaller than what you end up losing, many traders forget that they are placing their capital at risk. Make sure you come up with a ratio that will help protect your interests and then know how to manage trade risk.

No Privileges

When you use leverage to trade, you sacrifice full ownership of the asset. For instance, when you use leverage, you give up the opportunity of enjoying dividends. This is because the amount on the dividend is deducted from the account regardless of the position of the trade.

Margin Calls

A margin call is when the lender asks you to add funds so that you keep the trade open. You have to decide whether you wish to add funds or exit a position to reduce the exposure.

Incur Expenses

When you use leverage to trade options, you will receive the money from the lender so that you can use the full position. Most traders opt to keep their positions open overnight, which attracts a fee to cover the costs.

How Much Leverage Do You Need in Options Trading

Knowing how to trade options needs detailed knowledge about the various aspects of economics. For many people, the lack of knowledge to use leverage is the major cause of losses.

Studies show that many traders who opt for options lose money in the process. This happens whether for smaller or high leverage.

Risks of High Leverage

In options trading, the capital for placing a trade is usually sourced from a broker. While you have the ability to borrow huge amounts to place on a trade, you can gain more if the trade is successful.

A few years back, traders were able to offer leverages of up to 400 times the initial capital. However, rules and regulations have been, and at the moment, you can only access 50 times what you have. For instance, if you have $1000, you can control up to $50,000.

Choosing the Right Leverage

You need to look at different factors when choosing the kind of leverage that will work for you.

First, you need to start with low levels of leverage, because the more you borrow, the more you will need to pay back. Second, you need to use stops to make sure you protect the amount you have borrowed. Remember losses won't go down well with you.

All in all, you need to choose leverage which you find is comfortable for you. If you are a beginner, go for low leverage so that you minimize risks. If you know what you are doing, then go for maximum leverage to build your returns.

Using stops on order allows you to reduce loses when the trade changes direction. As a newbie, this is the only protection you need to make it in the market. This is because you will learn about the trades and how to place them while limiting any losses that might arise.

How to Manage Risk in Options Trading

Options trading come with a number of risks that you need to manage so that you can enjoy the profits and minimize losses.

Here are a few risks and how to deal with them.

Losing More than What You Have

This risk is inherent in options trading, especially if you are using leverage to make a trade. It means that you put up a small fraction of the initial deposit to open the trade. This means that your fate is in the hands of the direction of the market. If it goes along with your prediction, you will gain more than the deposit. On the other hand, if the direction changes and you lose the position, you might end up losing more than your initial deposit.

When this happens, you need to have a strategy in place to help mitigate the risk. What you need to do in this case is to set a limit, so that you define the exact level at which the trade should stop so that you don't lose more than you can handle.

Positions Closing Unexpectedly

When positions close unexpectedly, they lead to loss of money. To keep the trades open, you need to have some money in the account. This aspect is called the margin, and if you don't have enough funds to cover the margin, then the position might close.

To mitigate this, you need to keep an eye on the running balances and always add funds as needed.

Sudden Huge Losses or Gains

The market can turn out to be volatile, and when it does, you need to move fast. Markets change depending on the news or something else in the market, which can be an announcement, event, or changes in trader behavior.

Apart from having stops, you also need to get notifications regarding any upcoming movement, which tells you whether to react or not,

Orders Filled in Erroneously

When you give instructions to a broker to place a trade for you, and the broker instead does the opposite. This is termed slippage. When this happens, use guaranteed stops to make sure you protect yourself against any slippage that might occur.

How to Trade Smarter Using Leverage

Even with leverage in tow, you need to have a way to trade better. With many mistakes occurring during a trade, you stand to lose more than gain if you don't have the right tips to excel. Let us look at the top mistakes that you go through to get to the top.

Misunderstanding Leverage

Many beginners don't understand leverage and go ahead to misuse this feature, barely realizing the risk they are exposing themselves to.

To make this work for you, learn about leverage, and master it. Understand what it is and what it isn't and then find out the best ways to make use of it. You also need to understand how much you can put in without running huge losses.

Having No Exit Plan

Just like socks, you need to control your emotions when trading options. It doesn't mean that you have to swallow your greed and fear; rather, you need to have a plan that you can go with. Once you have a plan, you need to stick to it so that even when things aren't going your way, you have something to guide you to make a recovery.

You need to have an exit plan, which means you know when to drop a trade.

Failure to Try New Strategies

You need to make sure you try out a few new strategies depending on the level of trading you want to achieve. Most traders get a single strategy and then stick to it even when it is not working out for them. When this happens, you are often tempted to go against the rules that you set down.

Mistakes to Avoid in Options Trading

Trading is not an easy thing. Most of you do not know that. You just start the business with no plans, tips, and strategies. How do you even expect to survive? Entering into the options trading game with so much excitement, forgetting the crucial things you need to do will lead you nowhere. Mistakes eventually arise, and you become stranded on what to do. You will be informed of some of the mistakes traders commit and the ways you can shun from those mistakes.

Common Options Trading Mistakes

There are several common mistakes that traders commit while trading options. Below is a detailed list you can go through it.

Lacking a trading plan. Most traders enter into the options trading game without a plan. You have got a high potential for loss. Failure to organize you into trading is preparing to fail. Without guidelines, you cannot make it in trading. All your goals of making money will be destroyed. When you buy or sell that option, you will be incurring a lot of losses.

Lacking an exit strategy. When your plans fail to work out, what do you do? Do you just implement rushing decisions on your trading? An escape plan comes in handy here. Having an exit plan is very crucial in all trading. You can control your profits and losses. Most traders fail to have a detailed escape plan, which makes them fail tremendously. You lose all your money and fail in trading.

Having ignorance at the time of expiry. Options have a date of expiration. It is an important factor when purchasing calls and buying put options. Most traders fail to recognize this factor and end up messing up the last minute. Options lose their value when you are closer to the time of expiration.

Buying options with the mentality that they are cheap. Cheap is expensive. Cheap options have lower premiums compared to the expensive ones. You will earn little or no cash with cheap options with many losses. Options that are out of the money are not friendly at all, especially for beginners in options trading.

Selecting the wrong trade. Working on a trade that you cannot handle can land you into big trouble. There is a high potential for bigger risks. Work on the trade you can manage to succeed. Putting effort into complex stuff than your ability is a total failure. Many traders who get themselves on the wrong trade lose a lot of their money and precious time.

Depending on guesswork. Too much guesswork in options trading is a risky game. Guesswork like the rise and fall in the stock's price is not an advisable strategy. You should take advantage of the tools of research, analysis, and education materials. Tools for analysis help in analyzing outcomes in a detailed manner as compared to guesswork. Education materials will empower your knowledge a lot in trading, and you will be aware of the basic concepts. The research tool will assist in the formulation of strategies to be used in trading. The use of guesswork will surprise you a lot with the trading failures.

Ignoring protective stop loss. Failing to have a stop loss is a really bad idea. You can fail tremendously in trading. Most traders, who prefer to cheap options, wait to go out of the market when the option becomes fruitful, or it declines when it reaches the time of expiration.

Being over-optimistic. Optimism is always acceptable though being over-optimistic is another bad idea. Options trading are all about performing some mathematical calculations and coming up with the right figures for your returns and losses. Putting a positive mind always is not healthy in trading since many risks are involved here. You need to be prepared for the losses that might occur and be ready enough to handle them.

Using only one strategy. There exists some information about the many strategies you can implement in options trading. You need to go through the many strategies before deciding you will settle on which strategy. You not advised to rely on only one strategy. Having different strategies will help a lot. In case one trading strategy fails yet you are in a critical situation, you can implement another successful strategy as quickly as possible. Your trading will experience no delay. You should consider mostly the simple and crucial strategies that are needed to be implemented in all options trading. An example of the strategies is the covered call strategy.

Trading with a bigger bite. What's all with the rush? A successful money-making procedure requires smaller and sure moves other than big and weak moves. Take your time in trading and go at the right speed. Do not be so greedy for the money that you make complex decisions ending up losing everything. Good things take time. You need to accept that fact. When you utilize much of your cash, there are higher chances of bigger losses other than just spending a little money.

Lacking persistence and consistency. Trading is not like any other business that makes a huge amount of money just in the few days after entering the business. First and foremost, trading is tough and risky. You need to persist with all the risks and also be consistent. Most traders give up when there are occurrences of risks in trading. Keep pushing hard and of course, everything will work out fine.

Failing to accept uncertainties. All markets have imperfections. Failure to accept the things you cannot control in options trading is a big loss.

Market uncertainties will always be there, be ready to accept them and look for something else that you can control to save your time and money. Worrying a lot into something not useful is not advised in options trading.

Lacking trading goals. "By the time the year ends, I want to have…" These are the kinds of goals all options traders need to have. Who out there works out for things with no goals? Goals are the things we wish to have or do. Failure to have clear and realistic goals in options trading is a turn off to being successful in options trading. You need to have goals that you are working for. Traders who lack goals do not have the motivation to achieve something greater. Most of them do things for the sake of doing it. They trade at any time and use their money recklessly. Lacking goals leads to the failure of the options trading.

How to Avoid Common Mistakes

Mistakes are always in the game. You need to find yourself some strategies and ways to survive in options trading. Mistakes are part of the learning process. You should learn from your mistakes for growth and improvement the next time you are trading.

Do not be emotional when you commit mistakes in options trading. You will get carried away by the emotions and end up doing things of no importance. Go through your mistakes and see where you went wrong. Put much effort next time and avoid the mistakes to succeed.

Below is a detailed list of some of the ways on how to shun from common mistakes in options trading?

Possess an options trading plan. Test the plan after formulating it. If it works, it is well and good. Stick to it. It helps in organizing your trading patterns. You will be able to estimate your profits and losses. A trading plan makes you disciplined and responsible for trading. You will know your moves during your worst-case scenarios while trading options. Implement your working strategies according to the plan.

Work with a different and reasonable number of strategies. Do not rely on one strategy. It is dangerous. Arm yourself with several successful and crucial options trading strategies to be on the safer side when market imperfections decide to play along. Strategies assist you on how to do your things in trading and provide protective measures.

Take good advantage of technical tools provided to you by your broker. They enhance a quick understanding of options trading and understanding the basic concepts. They also ease the trading process since most of the trading platforms are online software.

Do not spend much money when placing trades, especially when you are a beginner. Begin from a small amount since the risks involved here are minimal. Do not utilize all your cash when you are a newbie only to end up losing everything. Take care of your money since you worked hard for it.

While trading, utilize the disposable income that can easily be refunded. Do not reach for your school fees or money for food. The risks involved in options trading are huge; it is tough to refund the money you lost. Using the money for food to placing trades will lead to starving and lack of school fees. Be wise when dealing with this trading.

You need to have realistic and achievable goals that you want to accomplish when starting off options trading. Goals are there to motivate you in trading. You will always put effort into trading to succeed what you desire.

Enter into a trade that you can manage. Many individuals will mislead you on the internet on the types of trades. Stick to your plans and select the types of trades good for you. Getting yourself into many and complex trades will stress you a lot.

There are different types of options such as binary options and many others. You should decide on the type of option you will settle with. Do not be the trader who deals with everything. Things will go out of control and you will lose everything. Decide on the option you more interested in and perfect that skill on the market.

Traders should be serious with the factor of time of expiration. The time of expiry is related to the value of an option. You should be alert and select options with a longer duration to expiry for your option to have a high value. You will be able to gain profits and massive returns.

Consider volatility in the market. It will save you from a lot of trouble in the market. The metric, implied volatility, can tell how volatile the market will be in the future. The metric can tell the amount of options premium you are capable of generating. You should, therefore, make use of the implied volatility in options trading.

Practice a lot in options trading. Have a routine of when to place your trades on the platforms. Study more on the best time to perform your type of trades in the options trading market. Practice will make you get used to trading with time which is a tip for successful options trading.

Have an escape plan for yourself. Do not start trading without an exit plan. This strategy saves you from losses when the market is experiencing worst-case scenarios. It guides you on the actions to implement at dark times which are better than the closure of a business.

Buying not-cheaper options are preferred to sticking to only cheaper options. Cheaper options have no progress in trading; they have lower options premiums as compared to the expensive ones. You should buy good options to earn more. Check on the quality of the options before purchasing.

Tend using protective measures in options trading. Measures such as covered call strategy assisting in protecting your trading capital and prevents you from risks in trading.

Analyzing Mood Swing in the Market

The market is a chaotic place with a number of traders vying for dominance over one another. There are a countless number of strategies and time frames in play and at any point; it is close to impossible to determine who will emerge with the upper hand. In such an environment, how is it then possible to make any money? After all, if everything is unpredictable, how can you get your picks right?

Well, this is where thinking in terms of probabilities comes into play. While you cannot get every single bet right, as long as you get enough right and make enough money on those to offset your losses, you will make money in the long run.

It's not about getting one or two right. It's about executing the strategy with the best odds of winning over and over again and ensuring that your math works out with regards to the relationship between your win rate and average win.

So, it really comes down to finding patterns which repeat themselves over time in the markets. What causes these patterns? Well, the other traders of course! To put it more accurately, the orders that the other traders place in the market are what creates patterns that repeat themselves over time.

The first step to understanding these patterns is to understand what trends and ranges are. Identifying them and learning to spot when they transition into one another will give you a massive leg up not only with your options trading but also with directional trading.

Trends

In theory spotting a trend is simple enough. Look left to right and if the price is headed up or down, it's a trend. Well, sometimes it is really that simple. However, for the majority of the time you have both with and counter-trend forces operating in the market. It is possible to have long counter trend reactions within a larger trend and sometimes, depending on the time frame you're in, these counter-trend reactions take up the majority of your screen space.

Trend vs Range

This is a chart of the UK100 CFD, which mimics the FTSE 100, on the four-hour time frame. Three-quarters of the chart is a downtrend and the last quarter is a wild uptrend. Using the looking left to right guideline; we'd conclude that this instrument is in a range. Is that really true though?

Just looking at that chart, you can clearly see that short-term momentum is bullish. So, if you were considering taking a trade on this, would you implement a range strategy or a trending one? This is exactly the sort of thing that catches traders up.

The key to deciphering trends is to watch for two things: counter trend participation quality and turning points. Let's tackle counter trend participation first.

Counter Trend Participation

When a new trend begins, the market experiences extremely imbalanced order flow which is tilted towards one side. There's isn't much counter trend participation against this seeming tidal wave of with trend orders. Price marches on without any opposition and experiences only a few hiccups.

As time goes on though, the with trend forces run out of steam and have to take breaks to gather themselves. This is where counter trend traders start testing the trend and trying to see how far back into the trend they can go. While it is unrealistic to expect a full reversal at this point, the quality of the correction or pushback tells us a lot about the strength distribution between the with and counter-trend forces.

Eventually, the counter-trend players manage to push so far back against the trend that a stalemate results in the market. The with and counter-trend forces are equally balanced and thus the trend comes to an end. After all, you need an imbalance for the market to tip one way or another and a balanced order flow is only going to result in a sideways market.

While all this is going on behind the scenes, the price chart is what records the push and pull between these two forces. Using the price chart, we can not only anticipate when a trend is coming to an end but also how long it could potentially take before it does. This second factor, which helps us estimate the time it could take, is invaluable from an options perspective, especially if you're using a horizontal spread strategy.

In all cases, the greater the number of them, the greater the counter-trend participation in the market. The closer a trend is to ending, the greater the counter-trend participation. Thus, the minute you begin to see price move into a large, sideways move with an equal number of buyers and sellers in it, you can be sure that some form of redistribution is going on.

Mind you, the trend might continue or reverse. Either way, it doesn't matter. What matters is that you know the trend is weak and that now is probably not the time to be banking on trend strategies.

Starting from the left, we can see that there is close to no counter trend bars, bearish in this case, and the bulls make easy progress. Note the angle with which the bulls proceed upwards.

Then comes the first major correction and the counter-trend players push back against the last third of the bull move. Notice how strong the bearish bars are and note their character compared to the bullish bars.

The bulls recover and push the price higher at the original angle and without any bearish presence, which seems odd. This is soon explained as the bears slam price back down and for a while, it looks as if they've managed to form a V top reversal in the trend, which is an extremely rare occurrence.

The price action that follows is a more accurate reflection of the power in the market, with both bulls and bears sharing chunks of the order flow, with overall order flow in the bull's favor but only just. Price here is certainly in an uptrend but looking at the extent of the bearish pushbacks, perhaps we should be on our guard for a bearish reversal. After all order flow is looking pretty sideways at this point.

So how would we approach an options strategy with the chart in the state it is in at the extreme right? Well, for one, any strategy that requires an option beyond the near month is out of the question, given the probability of it turning. Secondly, looking at the order flow, it does seem to be following a channel, doesn't it?

While the channel isn't very clean, if you were aggressive enough, you could consider deploying a collar with the strike prices above and below this channel to take advantage of the price movement. You could also employ some moderately bullish strategies as price approaches the bottom of this channel and figuring out the extent of the bull move is easier thanks to you being able to reference the top of the channel.

As price moves in this channel, it's all well and good. Eventually though, we know that the trend has to flip. How do we know when this happens?

Turning Points

As bulls and bears struggle over who gets to control the order flow, price swings up and down. You will notice that every time price comes back into the 6427-6349 zone, the bulls seem to step in masse and repulse the bears.

This tells us that the bulls are willing to defend this level in large numbers and strongly at that. Given the number of times the bears have tested this level, we can safely assume that above this level, bullish strength is a bit weak. However, at this level, it is as if the bulls have retreated and are treating this as a sort of last resort, for the trend to be maintained. You can see where I'm going with this.

If this level were to be breached by the bears, it is a good bet that a large number of bulls will be taken out. In martial terms, the largest army of bulls has been marshaled at this level. If this force is defeated, it is unlikely that there's going to be too much resistance to the bears below this level.

This zone, in short, is a turning point. If price breaches this zone decisively, we can safely assume that the bears have moved in and control the majority if the order flows.

Turning Point Breached

The decisive turning point zone is marked by the two horizontal lines and the price touches this level twice more and is repulsed by the bulls. Notice how the last bounce before the level breaks produces an extremely weak bullish bounce and price simply caves through this. Notice the strength with which the bears break through.

The FTSE was in a longer uptrend on the weekly chart, so the bulls aren't completely done yet. However, as far as the daily timeframe is concerned, notice how price retests that same level but this time around, it acts as resistance instead of support.

For now, we can conclude that as long as the price remains below the turning point, we are bearishly biased. You can see this by looking at the angle with which bulls push back as well as, the lack of strong bearish participation on the push upwards.

This doesn't mean we go ahead and pencil in a bull move and start implementing strategies that take advantage of the upcoming bullish move. Remember, nothing is for certain in the markets. Don't change your bias or strategy until the turning point decisively breaks.

Some key things to note here are that a turning point is always a major S/R level. It is usually a swing point where a large number of with trend forces gather to support the trend. This will not always be the case, so don't make the mistake of hanging on to older turning points.

The current order flow and price action are what matters the most, so pay attention to that above all else. Also, note how the candles that test this level all have wicks on top of them.

This indicates that the bears are quite strong here and that any subsequent attack will be handled the same way until the level breaks. Do we know when the level will break? Well, we can't say with any accuracy. However, we can estimate the probability of it breaking.

The latest upswing has seen very little bearish pushback, comparatively speaking, and the push into the level are strong. Instinct would say that there's one more rejection left here. However, who knows? Until the level breaks, we stay bearish. When the level breaks, we switch to the bullish side.

Putting it all Together

So now we're ready to put all of this together into one coherent package. Your analysis should always begin with determining the current state of the market. Ranges are pretty straightforward to spot, and they occur either within big pullbacks in trends or at the end of trends.

Trends vary in strength depending on the amount of counter-trend participation they have. The way to determine counter trend participation levels is to simply look at the price bars and compare the counter-trend ones to the with trend ones. The angle with which the trend progresses is a great gauge as well, for its strength, with steeper angles being stronger.

You need to determine the turning point of the trend. The turning point is a level that is extremely well defended by the with trend players and will be attacked repeatedly by the counter-trend traders in long trends.

Technical Analysis and Its Basics

No matter the kind of vehicle you choose for your actions, there are some basics that you have to be familiar with. This fundamental knowledge is mostly connected to the behavior of the markets. If you learn how to recognize the way they behave, you will be able to anticipate the movement of the prices more accurately, thus make smarter decisions while trading. It can be interesting to note that regardless of the value that is traded on the market, some concepts can always apply to the prices and their way of performance on the market.

This can be explained by independent traders and investors being responsible for short-term price fluctuations. We can say that the price depends on the actions of the people who invest or trade values on the market and those prices react in a similar way when they are given similar input or stimuli. The study that is dedicated to researching the ways of price behavior is called technical analysis and understanding its basic is one of the most essential education points that you will need to be able to make correct financial decisions on the market.

The Basics of Technical Analysis

Technical analysis represents a huge topic. If you decide to enter the market and become an investor, there is a high possibility that you will catch yourself coming back to studying and learning something new many times for as long as you intend to work as a trader. That is why every person knowledgeable in options trading would advise that a basic understanding of technical analysis is a very important step for every person involved in the market. However, you don't need to know everything about it right away. Since it is a large area of research, it is ok if for some aspects of your business you just research parts of the technical analysis that you are particularly interested in for that concrete project. For instance, the technical analysis offers more than a hundred indicators for analyzing the market. In reality, traders usually use three or four, mostly the most popular ones or just those that they were familiar within the first place.

If you don't limit yourself only to option trading but you do trading in general, you will realize that technical analysis can be applied to any financial instruments such as futures or stocks for example.

We can say that their basis is in psychology and human nature in general and how they behave in practice. For better understanding, we will overview some of the main topics in technical analysis. These topics will be:

Technical analysis' foundation; how to chart principles and trends; patterns in technical analysis; technical analysis through the movement of the averages, and Indicators in technical analysis.

Technical analysis' foundation

The main basis of the technical analysis is found in the term known as " market action". Market action represents a whole personal knowledge about the trading market, and it doesn't include information that you might obtain from an insider. It can be simply defined as a study that determines: "the way that the price moves over time". If possible, it also examines its volumes and how they change over time too.

Still, the fundamental concept of technical analysis is based on the premise that the behavior of the market is a reflection of everything that happened and will happen with the price at a certain moment. Many things can have an impact on the price, and the amount of the impact depends on the market in which the trade is made. That's where technical analysis comes in, it cuts across all of those possibilities and states that all the things that can be known about the price are basically already included in the price that we see at the moment we want to trade.

This means that you shouldn't worry too much about the things that influence the price, as according to this it is enough to follow how the price changes over time and you will get all your answers. At first, many people wondered if this kind of principle can work because it sounded rather easy. If you had any doubts, the answer was already proven and it says that yes, technical analysis is successful although this kind of definition doesn't seem that complicated.

However, there is one very important point coming out from all of this. Technical analysis doesn't guarantee the behavior of the price. It can tell you that the price will increase or decrease for a certain period, but that doesn't necessarily happen. It may or it may not. The reason for this is that regardless of the calculation that the market has to do something, it is impossible to be 100 percent sure that it will. The market has its own ways and eventually does what it wants. So what technical analysis does is that it gives you the indication that shows what will be the most probable outcome, which means that the only certainty that you get is to know if the law of probability is on your side or not.

You can do a large number of average trades and hopefully make some profit, but you should never invest an amount of money or some valuable goods such as your house or your car if you can't afford to lose it. It is not recommended especially if one successful trade makes you confident that just one is enough to be a good technical indicator for certain gain. This is one of the reasons why the first task of technical analysis is to improve your chance for success by analyzing the prices and the way they behave on the market.

The second reason for the analysis is the fact that prices almost always change using certain trends. For instance, if the price increases its trend will be to rise until there is something that disables it from further growth. In comparison, we can say that prices act like Newton's motion law, which says that: "a body in motion will stay in motion unless acted upon by an external force." Of course, to prove this to be true, it has to happen over time. If this weren't the case the price charts represented in many analyses wouldn't be the way they are. They would be illustrated as a random movement of the prices. The third reason is that technical analysis supposes that history will, as always, repeat itself. If certain situations happened in the past, and you see them happening once again in the present than it is highly expected that the same thing will happen in the future too. Since people are not expected to change in this equation, the second logical conclusion would be that their results will be the same too. In a nutshell- this was a very foundation of technical analysis. Don't forget that one of the most efficient ways to become good in trading and to increase your chance to become a successful investor is to be able to use most of the things that this analysis can give you.

There are a few arguments that you can hear against the use of technical analysis. Still, the only proof that you really need is the fact that this analysis works and that at least it can improve your chances to get more percentages while trading. However, we will point out some of the attitudes toward technical analysis:

One of the traders said: "Charts only show what has happened in the past, how they can reveal what hasn't happened yet?" The answer to this is quite simple, there is evidence from earlier trades and those pieces of evidence are used in technical analysis with the premise that history will repeat itself. This way you can anticipate at least with some fair certainty what is the next thing that will happen with the price on the market. In comparison, it works in a similar way as the weather forecast, if they say that it will rain on the TV, you know that it might not rain even though they said it will, but you take your umbrella with you anyway. The same principle applies with the technical analysis and that is how you can predict the future by using the past events.

Another trader noted: "If the prices already incorporate everything there is to know, then any change in price can only come from new information that we don't know yet." This kind of idea doesn't only appear in trading options, it is present in all financial markets. It surfaces in many areas and even academics are still discussing it. Differently, from the opinion that is popular between the traders, this concept doesn't actually say that the price that is currently on the market is the correct one. It just states that it isn't possible to establish if that current price is too low or too high. That is why the smartest choice to deal with this concept is to prove in which way technical analysis really works. In the end, if everyone supported this kind of idea then we would have zero analysis and the price would be always the same. We can imply that technical analysis has self-fulfilling characteristics.

This means that if the majority of traders do the analysis and estimate that the price has to increase all of them would become buyers on the market, which would mean an increase in demand, thus price that went up. The same principle applies to the price that is supposed to go down. This is one more example in which technical analysis showed that it works. Of course, there can always be some doubts but does it really matter to prove why the price went in the direction that you thought it would? Additionally, if a large number of traders who are not well educated and they just want to make quick profit fail, it can be seen as a sort of evidence that the idea of having a massive amount of traders regardless of their knowledge and dedication is somehow wrong from the beginning.

How to chart principles and trends

After we have seen what the basic principles of the technical analysis are, it is time to see how the prices are charted or graphed and what those graphs mean. There is no way of escaping this even though some might find it unnecessary. You will be forced to see this kind of chart during your whole trading career. It is easier to understand these principles if you go slowly, step by step and try to remember how these principles work. There are few diverse types of the chart but all of them mostly use horizontal bottom and timescale as a vertical scale.

The price is usually up to the side, and for someone who is just starting, these charts are the only ones that you should be interested in. The vertical line or the timescale can be expressed in minutes, in days, or even weeks, so you will look at the one, which is suitable for your trading style. However, it is not unusual that you'd want to know what happens with the other time scales as long as they are around the values you chose. Experienced traders mostly look at the other time scales to get the bigger picture on what's happening on the market. Here, we will mention three kinds of charts and we will suppose that they all have the same time vertical line and that they are all in the same currency.

Control Your Emotions

Since trading options is mostly about short time periods, most people have this idea that the prices of options are not going to fluctuate much in that time. But that is wrong, and you need to rethink if you are thinking along those lines as well. If you study past data, you will see that options trading witnesses a lot of fluctuations in price even if it is over a short period of time. So, if you think that options trading mean your money will stay protected, then I have to tell you that you are wrong. Of course, people lose money in options trading, just like investing directly in the stock market. But that does not mean you have to be happy about the fact you are losing money because you will feel low and you will start panicking – that is the NORMAL reaction. But you have to learn how to keep your emotions in check.

You need to learn how to remain calm and observe your emotions from a distance instead of giving in to them. Slowly, you will learn how you can stick it out so that you can see whether or not you get any good returns in the future before the expiration date. Options trading can really be a financial roller coaster. You cannot invest in options with the mentality of a Warren Buffet investor because options do not appreciate in the same manner. A little bit of study would reveal that options increase on a percentage basis, and their movement is way faster than any other type of investment.

For example, if a person has multiple contracts in his/her possession and is trading them all, then they might incur simultaneous losses and profits of $500 each over the course of a few hours. But technically speaking, do not confuse options traders with day traders because they are not, but your mindset should be slightly like that of a day trader if you want to make it big in options trading.

I am going to show you how you can control your emotions even when you are on this rollercoaster ride of options trading.

Getting Started

As a beginner, you will have a tendency to jump into the market right away and begin your journey as a trader. But before you do that, let me remind you of some of the things that are crucial for you to learn. I cannot stress enough on the fact that a good and proper understanding of the basics of options trading is going to get you far in your journey. You also should learn about the different types of options that are present in the market so that you know what you should pick. I know that I have probably told you all of this before, but I am reiterating this for one simple reason, and that is – this is the golden rule about being a top trader. The more you enhance your knowledge about investing, the more will be your chances to get success.

Once you have gone through all the basics and understood them carefully, you will have a clear picture in your head about what you are getting yourself into. The next step is to find your motivation and always hold tightly to it because, in trading, beginners tend to lose that motivation very fast. You need to ask yourself exactly how much money do you think about making. The figure will vary from person to person, and although there is no limit to this, you should still be realistic about it. No one becomes a billionaire overnight. You should also ask yourself how you plan to spend or use that money once you have earned it. This is where you are going to find your motivation because you are setting goals or you have some dreams that you want to fulfill, and so you will try your best to make those dreams come true. When you are in the thick of the trading, this motivation is going to keep you going and also help you stay focused on the trade.

When you have the trading plan ready, it will constantly tell you about the things that you should achieve in a trade. Some of the common things that are included in a trading plan are – your goals, your idea of what is going to happen, the strategies that you want to use, and any other note or guideline that you think might be of use to you. All of this together is going to make you successful. You will be putting yourself into a risky endeavor if you start trading without having this plan ready.

Never Make Emotional Decisions

As you must have understood by now that options are very volatile in nature, and depending on certain stocks, it can get really very volatile. There are so many beginner traders who come into options trading but then become emotional because it is not what they thought it would be. And this is exactly what I am talking about. This approach will not do any good to you, and that is why prior research is necessary to know the waters you are stepping into.

In most cases, people exit at the wrong time just because they became emotional and overwhelmed during the trade, but only if they had stayed a bit longer or if they had made their exit a bit early, they would have been able to make a lump sum profit. If you are trading options, your worst mistake would be to make any sudden moves. That is why a trading plan is so necessary so that you can have all the rules at hand on when do you need to exit or enter a trade. And all you have to do is stick to those rules.

The tides in the financial market keep changing, and if you want to navigate them like a pro, then active monitoring is important. There will come a time when you will feel like giving in to your behavioral impulses, but you have to stop yourself right there and take a step back to analyze the situation in front of you. The market ups and downs can easily make you start practicing emotional buying and selling if you are not careful. And the usual trend shows that whenever the market is good, investors have the tendency of piling into investments and then they sell at the bottom. This is mostly because of the fear and hype generated by media.

There are several theories that have been proposed about investor behavior because it is something that is being studied extensively. But if we look at the real-life situation, you will understand that trading can bring about stress, and in situations of extreme stress, it is quite common for rational thinking to be clouded by the investor's psyche. The stress can not only be a result of panic but also euphoria. That is why I have told you time and again that the approach towards investing should be realistic and rational. Never underestimate risk management because every investment has its own risks, and if you do not gauge those risks, then you are the one who will be at a loss.

There are so many non-professional investors in the market who actually use their hard-earned money for trading just because they think they are going to receive a huge return. But sometimes market developments can lead them to lose their money, and it is very painful indeed. All of this leads to extreme stress and that stress, in turn, can lead to second-guessing every step. That is why you need to identify what your risk tolerance is so that you do not end up making emotional decisions when these risks become unbearable for you.

Be a Bit Math-Oriented

If you are not good with numbers or if you are shy about it, then you are not going to do well in options trading. This is because it is entirely a game of numbers. But don't get me wrong, I am not asking you to go to some renowned university to get a degree in mathematics or statistics.

You can read a bit by yourself and get a grasp on the basic concepts because a little bit of knowledge about statistics and probability will do you good in the long term and make you better than the others in the world of options trading. To be honest, I don't know how you are going to get to the top if you do not know the basics of statistics. The core of options trading will always have some Maths in it, and you cannot go around it in any way.

Also, when you are math-oriented, you will have a better understanding of the market, and you will see options in a different light. You will learn to analyze the situations and markets before going all-in with your capital. This, in turn, will also make strategizing an easier process.

Maintain Trading Journals

When you have a trading journal, keeping track of your trade becomes way easier. Your brokerage statement is not going to include everything, whereas your trading journal will have all those details, making it easier for you. It will also remind you of the mistakes you made in a certain market condition. Do you know how this is going to benefit you? If that same market condition were to repeat itself, you know exactly what strategy you will not be using, and this will help you not to make the same mistake again. You can also keep track of every time you became emotional and what triggered you. This is will not prevent you from becoming emotional but it will remind you of the loss you incurred and this probably will help you get a grip on yourself.

When you record your trades and make notes in your journal, you get a clear picture of the situation you are in. Yes, sometimes, that picture can be wrong, and this does not mean that you have to back out. A losing record is simply when you have to find out where you are going wrong and why you are not making profits from the trade. All of this will become easier because you have written your steps in the trading journal. And then all you have to make is adjustments.

Conclusion

They can be extremely profitable but learning to trade them well takes time. You can choose to use indicators to determine your entry points, and I'm all for this approach at first but remembers that over the long term, you're better served learning the basics of order flow and using that.

There is no shortage of options strategies you can use to limit your risk and depending on the volatility levels dramatically; you can deploy separate strategies to achieve the same ends. Contrast this with a directional trading strategy where you have just one method of entry, which is to either go short or go long, and only one way of managing risk, which is to use a stop loss.

Spread or market neutral trading puts you in the position of not having to care about what the market does. In addition, it brings another dimension of the market into focus, which is volatility. Volatility is the greatest thing for your gains and options allow you to take full advantage of this, no matter what the volatility situation currently is.

Options can be a bit hard to get your head around at first since so many of us are used to looking at the market as a thing that goes up or down. Options bring a sideways and a different vertical element to it via spreads and volatility estimates. More advanced options strategies take full advantage of volatility and are more math-focused, so if this interests you, you should go for them.

That being said, do not assume the complexity means more gains. They bring you the advantage of leverage without having to borrow a single cent.

You can choose to borrow, of course, but you need to do this only if it is in line with your risk management math. Risk management is what will make or break your results and at the center of quantitative risk management is your risk per trade. Keep this consistent and line up your success rate and reward to risk ratios, and you'll make money as a mathematical certainty.

Qualitative risk management requires you to adopt the right mindset with regards to trading, and it is crucial for you to adopt this as quickly as possible. Remember that the implications of your risk math mean that you need not be concerned with the outcome of a single trade. Instead, seek to maximize your gains over the long term.

The learning curve might get steep at times, but given the rewards on offer, this is a small price to pay. Keep hammering away at your skills, and soon you'll find yourself trading options profitably, and everything will be worth it. How much can you expect to make trading options?

Generally, a good options trade can expect around 50-80% returns on their capital. As you grow in size, this return amount will decrease naturally.

I wish you the best of luck in all of your trading efforts. The key to success is to simply never give up and to be resilient. Reduce the stress on yourself, and you'll be fine. Here's wishing you all the success in your options trading journey!